Crime Control in Ireland: The Poli
of Intolerance

UNDERCURRENTS

Other titles in the series

UNDERCURRENTS    Series Editor Carol Coulter

# Crime Control in Ireland: The Politics of Intolerance

IAN O'DONNELL AND
EOIN O'SULLIVAN

CORK UNIVERSITY PRESS

First published in 2001 by
Cork University Press
University College
Cork
Ireland

**British Library Cataloguing in Publication Data**
A CIP catalogue record for this book is available from
the British Library

ISBN 1 85918 274 7

Typeset by Tower Books, Ballincollig, Co. Cork
Printed and bound by CPI Antony Rowe, Eastbourne

# Contents

# Acknowledgements

The authors would like to acknowledge the assistance they received from the following: Carol Coulter, Greg Heylin, Paddy Hillyard, Bill Lockhart, Niamh Maguire, Jarlath McKee, Eddie O'Donnell, Kieran O'Dwyer, Tom O'Malley, Barry Vaughan and Peter Young.

None of the above, of course, bears any responsibility for the views expressed in this book, which are those of the authors alone.

# 1. Introduction

In June 1980, in an IMS survey for *The Irish Times*, members of the public were asked what they thought was the most important problem facing the country.[1] Only seven per cent put crime at the top of their list. Eight years later, a similar question was asked in an IMS survey for Independent Newspapers. Only two per cent were of the view that crime and issues of law and order were the most important problems facing the country.[2] Six years on, in 1994, in a survey conducted for *The Sunday Press*, three per cent believed that crime was the most important issue facing the country.[3]

Remarkably, just two years later, in 1996, when asked to identify the most critical issue facing the government, nearly 50 per cent chose crime and law and order.[4] In the same survey, 88 per cent thought the government was losing the fight against crime, a figure that dropped to 62 per cent a number of months later.[5] At the beginning of 1997, when asked whether crime rates were increasing, continuing at the same level as previous years or declining, 86 per cent responded that crime was increasing.[6] Suddenly, concern about crime had become a national priority.[7]

There is no neat relationship between public anxiety and the crime rate. In 1980, the official figure for indictable crime stood at 72,782. This represented 2,140 crimes for every 100,000 persons living in the country, and was a 236 per cent increase on the 1970 figure, which in turn was a doubling of the 1960 figure. Three years later, in 1983, for the first time in the history of the State, more than 100,000 indictable crimes were recorded by the Garda (a rate of 2,922 crimes per 100,000 population). This figure dropped below 100,000 crimes for each of the next ten years, averaging 91,571 crimes per annum between 1984 and 1993.

In 1994, however, when only three per cent of the public thought crime was the most serious issue facing the country, the number of crimes exceeded 100,000, with similar figures for 1995 and 1996. In 1997, when 86 per cent of those surveyed in an *Irish Times* poll were of the view that crime was increasing, the official figure dropped by a remarkable 10,000 to 90,875, a pattern of decrease that has continued to the present. In 1999, just over 80,000 indictable crimes were recorded by the Garda, the lowest level for 20 years.

The current Minister for Justice, Equality and Law Reform, John O'Donoghue, has taken credit for much of this decrease in crime, arguing that his emphasis on the triple lock of 'zero tolerance' policing, new criminal justice legislation and massive expansion of the prison system, has made the streets safer.

O'Donoghue had been vitriolic in opposition, berating the then Minister for Justice, Nora Owen of Fine Gael, for presiding over a growing crime rate, allowing serious criminals to stalk the streets with impunity and continuing the practice of large-scale temporary release to ease the pressures of prison overcrowding.

Although overall crime rates began to fall in 1995, the same year saw a near doubling in the number of murders. This contributed to an escalation in fear of crime. The sudden surge in homicide was not simply a statistical fluctuation, and has been sustained in recent years.

Public concern was inflated by increasingly aggressive reporting of crime issues by the media, leading to the belief that gardaí were unable to deal with a small number of individuals who were thought to control organised crime and the drug trade in Dublin. Frustration grew alongside increasing media coverage of the key figures and their lavish lifestyles.

Demands for action escalated with the killing of a Garda detective on 7 June 1996. Jerry McCabe was shot dead during an attempted robbery of a post office van in Adare. Two weeks later the investigative journalist Veronica Guerin was murdered as she sat in her car in Dublin traffic. At a time of increasing concern about serious crime, these two murders brought matters to a head.

These killings were defining moments in the debate about law and order in Ireland. They were the catalyst for a hardening in political attitudes. Crime control became a national priority and it was almost as if a state of national emergency had been declared. The Dáil was recalled for a special debate, and during the 1997 general election campaign, law and order were key issues and public concern seemed to be at an all-time high. Politicians engaged in a frenzied bidding war, promising more gardaí, more prisons and less tolerance.

This was a textbook case of a 'moral panic', a term coined by the sociologist Stan Cohen to define a situation in which,

> A condition, episode, person or group of persons emerges to become defined as a threat to societal values and interests; its nature is presented in a stylized and stereotypical fashion by the mass media; the moral barricades are manned by editors, bishops, politicians and other right-thinking people ... Sometimes the panic passes over and is forgotten ... at other times it has more serious and long-lasting repercussions and might produce such changes as those in legal and social policy or even in the way society conceives itself.[8]

The killings of Jerry McCabe and Veronica Guerin led to a period of moral panic that inflamed public anger and anxiety (as shown by the opinion poll results) and led to a raft of legal and policy changes, numerous column inches of newsprint and even a film. They were the occasion for a clampdown on 'organised' crime and threw up serious questions about the state's ability to police itself, about the extent to which there was a 'control deficit'. This was a very worrying scenario for many people and generated the conditions in which a harsh response to perceived lawlessness became acceptable.

Fianna Fáil, in opposition at the time, promised a policy of 'zero tolerance'. By this they meant that, 'No crime, no matter how small, is insignificant; tolerance of small crimes creates a climate where big crimes flourish; and there is a certain connection between lesser and more serious crimes.'[9] They argued for an increase in Garda numbers, restrictions on access to bail, mandatory sentences for 'drug peddlers and drug pushers' and an additional 2,000 prison places. If returned to government,

Fianna Fáil promised to 'give the streets of this country back to the Irish people'. Since their return to power in June 1997 (in coalition with the Progressive Democrats), Fianna Fáil have enthusiastically delivered on these election promises.

There have been previous occasions when the political mood hardened swiftly. For example, when recorded crime was heading for a peak in 1983, the Fine Gael TD for Louth, Brendan McGahon, was unequivocal: 'The problem of crime has got out of hand in most of the country . . . the people demand strong government. They do not expect economic miracles or to see the unemployment situation dramatically altered. But they demand and expect a reasonable level of law and order.'[10] The same year a statutory instrument was introduced to allow more than one prisoner per cell. For the first time, prison overcrowding became possible. The Criminal Justice Act 1984 enhanced a range of Garda powers and introduced consecutive sentences for offences committed on bail. It also doubled (to two years) the maximum sentence available to the District Court.

While many lawyers and civil libertarians viewed these measures as draconian,[11] they were followed by a substantial decrease in recorded crime. Although short-lived, this decrease never received the attention it deserved. It is an example of the glaring gaps in our knowledge about the criminal justice system, which Tom O'Malley has argued 'remains bedevilled by the absence of reliable and up-to-date statistical information'.[12]

Our key objectives in this book are to explore recent trends in crime in Ireland, drawing on the international evidence, and to investigate some of the ramifications of 'zero tolerance' politics as it has become part of the programme for government. The main thrust of our argument can be summarised as follows:

1. There was a marked reduction in recorded crime between 1995 and 1999. This conceals an increase in offences against the person.

2. The search for the 'true' level of crime is futile, although crime surveys provide a useful point of contrast with official sources of data.

3. Too much can be made of the statistics relating to one year in isolation. Crime data are only of value when considered as a time series. Similarly, it is impossible to draw meaningful inferences from short-term fluctuations in a single offence category.

4. The decline in recorded crime began *before* the current government came into power in June 1997. Therefore the fall in crime preceded the introduction of 'zero tolerance' measures and cannot be attributed to them.

5. The causes of crime are complex and shifting and are influenced more by social, economic and cultural forces than criminal justice policies.

6. While calls for 'zero tolerance' are unlikely to prevent much crime, they may influence the nature of policing. This can be seen in the surge in the number of proceedings taken against beggars, prostitutes and the disorderly public.

7. 'Zero tolerance' politics can influence the penal system in a concrete way. Ireland stands out in an international context not only for its low crime level, but also for the sudden expansion in its prison population.

8. Many conventional sociological predictors would appear to have limited value in explaining why crime has fallen in recent years.

9. The role of the economy seems critical. One consequence of more widespread legal opportunities for gain is a reduction in the attractiveness of illegal alternatives.

It must be acknowledged at the outset that recent developments have not been uniformly punitive and repressive. A striking characteristic of law and order politics since 1997 has been its inherent contradictions. As well as more repressive laws, more Gardaí and more prisons, there is more diversion of young people from prosecution,[13] more mediation[14] and more crime prevention.[15] As well as more custody (2,000 extra prison places), there is less custody (the Children Bill 1999 proposes detention as a last resort for those aged under 18). As well as more treatment for drug offenders (Drug Courts are being introduced on a pilot basis),[16] there is more punishment for drug offenders (the Criminal Justice Act 1999 provides mandatory minimum ten-year prison terms for possession of drugs valued at £10,000 or more).

This inconsistency is typical of modern societies searching for effective ways of tackling crime. Contemporary criminal justice practices and policies are inherently volatile and incoherent.[17] These contradictions and inconsistencies are central to this book.

# 2. The Rise and Fall of Crime

## Policing Irish Society

Our understanding of the concept of policing in Ireland is usually restricted to the activity of the Garda Síochána. Indeed it is the number of events reported to them, deemed criminal and recorded, that determines the rate of crime. However, this understanding is much narrower than earlier views, which encompassed a greater range of regulatory bodies.[18] In contemporary Irish society a range of agencies 'police' aspects of our behaviour. For example, the Health and Safety Authority regulates safety standards and penalises those individuals or agencies that are in breach. During 1998 and 1999 there were 40 fatalities in the construction industry in Ireland, with the largest proportion due to falls from heights on building sites.[19] In 1997, a High Court judge, Peter Kelly, was compelled to describe one of the largest construction companies in the country as a 'recidivist criminal'. He noted that the fines previously imposed by courts 'did not amount to so much as a fleabite to your profits and you were happy to pay them'. He added: 'You are entitled to make profits on the sweat of your workers, but you are not entitled to make profit on the blood and lives of your workers.'[20]

The Department of Social, Community and Family Affairs polices those who are in receipt of various social security allowances and penalises those who obtain such payments fraudulently.[21] The Revenue Commissioners have responsibility for ensuring compliance with the various Finance Acts that determine our tax liability. In 1998, 52,277 enforcement certificates were issued by the Revenue Commissioners, with a face value of £225m, while the number of cases referred for enforcement by court proceedings was 3,588.[22] The Department of Agriculture, Food and Rural Development has a role in food safety. Local authorities have considerable powers to evict and penalise tenants of their estates who are deemed to be anti-social.[23] We also have a growing private security industry with between 8,650 and 10,900 employees and an annual turnover of in excess of £200m.[24] Security guards are a very visible presence today in pubs, clubs, shops and financial institutions.

Thus, a number of agencies other than the Garda take responsibility for regulating or policing behaviour in Irish society, and only in some cases are rule-breakers dealt with by the criminal justice system. Despite the often overlooked importance of these agencies, it is the Garda Síochána that has primary responsibility for managing crime. Founded in 1922, its first commissioner, Michael Staines, claimed they would achieve their objectives 'not by force of arms or numbers but on their moral authority as servants of the people'.[25] Despite this founding principle, the number of gardaí has increased by over 70 per cent since 1960, giving Ireland a comparatively high number of police personnel per head of population, as is shown in Table 1.[26] The current government is on target to increase the number of gardaí by nine per cent between 1997 and 2002. This will move Ireland closer to the upper end of the European league table.

TABLE 1: Number of Police Personnel per 1,000 Population, 1997[27]

| | | | |
|---|---|---|---|
| Spain | 1.3 | **Ireland** | 3.0 |
| Finland | 1.5 | South Africa | 3.1 |
| Denmark | 1.9 | Germany | 3.1 |
| Switzerland | 2.0 | Greece | 3.7 |
| Australia | 2.0 | Scotland | 3.8 |
| England & Wales | 2.5 | Portugal | 4.6 |
| Sweden | 2.6 | Northern Ireland | 6.8 |

Source: *Sixth Survey on Crime Trends and the Operations of Criminal Justice Systems*, (United Nations, 2000)

## The Amount of Crime

The primary source of information on the incidence of crime in Ireland is the Garda Síochána Annual Report, which has been published continuously since 1947.[28] It is from this report that we obtain both the official extent of crime (that is crimes reported to and recorded by the Garda), and the official rate of sanctioning (that is conviction rates within a given year). The official crime rate can be understood as the number of officially recognised criminal acts as interpreted, mediated and published by the Garda.[29]

What constitutes a crime and how certain behaviour becomes defined as criminal has been a long-standing concern of criminologists.[30] For most people, crime is whatever the law deems to be illegal, but this restricts our understanding to the definitions provided by the State. However we define crime, we must always be conscious of why it is that only certain actions are deemed criminal and why only certain offences are criminally prosecuted. Crime is a socially and politically constructed concept that is forever shifting. For example, in a well-known essay, Herman and Julia Schwendinger argued that the right to racial, sexual and economic equality were basic and fundamental because there was so much at stake in their fulfilment. Following from this logic, they argued that if social relationships and social structures caused the systematic abrogation of basic rights, this should be classified as criminal.[31] Similarly, the thoughtful, but much neglected, Department of Justice discussion paper, *Tackling Crime*, published in 1997, noted that while most people would view murder, rape and so forth as serious crimes,

> There is some ambivalence, however, when it comes to other forms of wrongful behaviour, despite the fact that existing law may define such behaviour as serious criminal activity and prescribe penalties to match that categorisation. Some examples are driving while under the influence of drink, tax evasion and fraud. Driving

while under the influence of drink provides a particularly good example of this ambivalence. Although the
indications are that this form of offending probably
claims more lives than most others there is, at times, a
tendency to look upon those who offend not so much
as offenders, but as victims of unfortunate circumstances, especially if no harm is caused to person or
property.[32]

The Garda report separates crime into two classes, indictable
and non-indictable. In essence, the difference between them is
that non-indictable crimes are heard at the District Court only,
whereas indictable offences, because they are generally viewed
as more serious, can or must be dealt with before a judge and
jury.[33] While, in general terms, indictable offences are the most
serious, this is not always the case. For example, it may be
argued that some assaults (non-indictable, 9,471 in 1999),
dangerous driving (non-indictable, 3,865 in 1999) and public
disorder (non-indictable, 30,993 in 1999) are more serious than
larceny from unattended vehicles (indictable, 9,014 in 1999),
larceny of pedal cycles (indictable, 163 in 1999) or obstructing
clergy during services (indictable, 0 in 1999). It should be noted
that a detailed breakdown of the categories of indictable crime
for 1999 is only available for the first nine months due to a
changeover in the Garda computer system.[34]

There are also a number of hybrid categories; most notably
crimes related to the sale and distribution of illicit drugs. These
offences are classified on a case-by-case basis and at the discretion of the prosecution are tried as either indictable or
non-indictable offences. Since 1994, the majority of drug-related
offences have been classified separately and are not counted as
indictable or non-indictable offences.

The other key difference between indictable and non-
indictable crime is the manner in which the data are presented
in the Garda Annual Report. All indictable offences reported to
and recorded by the Garda are included in the report, whereas
for non-indictable crime, only reported cases in which

proceedings were taken are recorded. In one of the first detailed analyses of crimes figures in Ireland, published in 1980, it was argued that 'The format of the report is now anachronistic and in need of revision'[35]. To this day, however, it remains recognisably a product of nineteenth-century British police recording practices and social priorities.

## Recent Trends

In 1960 a total of 15,375 indictable crimes was recorded by the Garda. The vast majority were categorised as offences against property without violence. There were four murders (two of infants under one year of age), 337 cases of assault, wounding and other like offences, 116 indecent assaults on females and 70 other sexual offences. There were 6,580 gardaí, giving a rate of 2.3 crimes during the year for every garda.[36] In addition to these indictable offences, 102,795 persons had proceedings taken against them for non-indictable offences. Around three-quarters of these cases involved the Highway Acts.

The crime rate, which had remained remarkably consistent from the foundation of the state, started to increase very significantly from the late 1960s. This trend is shown in Figure 1.

By 1983, 102,387 indictable offences were recorded. For the first time, the critical threshold of 100,000 was broken. This represented 2,922 crimes per 100,000 members of the population. Of these recorded crimes, over half were against property and did not involve violence. There were 26 murders and 11 attempts to murder. A further 729,307 non-indictable offences were proceeded with. This peak year was followed by a steady reduction which persisted until 1987. Over this four-year period, there was a cumulative reduction of 17 per cent.

The rate began to rise again from the early 1990s, reaching its highest point ever in 1995, since when it has declined significantly. The cumulative reduction between 1995 and 1999 was 21 per cent. In the space of 20 years, crime has twice peaked and fallen sharply. The country is now at a low point in the cycle.

Figure 1: Indictable Crime, 1960–1999

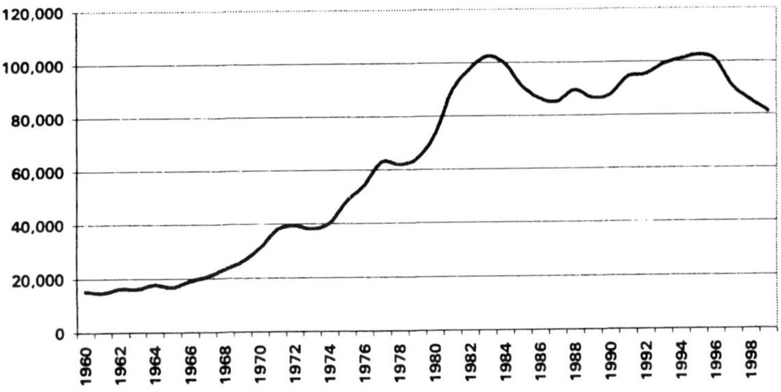

Source: Garda Síochána Annual Reports

In the full year 1999, 81,274 indictable offences were reported to and recorded by the Garda, a decrease of over five per cent on 1998. This represented 2,241 recorded crimes per 100,000 members of the population. There were 11,458 gardaí, giving us a rate of seven crimes during 1999 for every garda.

As O'Connell has pointed out, if account is taken of recent demographic changes in Ireland, which have led to a substantial increase in the population, the result is a more marked drop in the rate of indictable crime.[37] Figure 2 shows the rate of crime per 100,000 population. It would appear that the decline in crime highlighted by the Garda statistics in recent years is a significant underestimate.

During the first half of the 1960s, the official detection rate fluctuated between 50 per cent and a remarkable 70 per cent (see Figure 3). From then on it plummeted, dropping to just over 30 per cent for most of the 1980s. It has been slowly increasing since the early 1990s, with a slight dip in 1999. In terms of solving crimes, the gardaí appear to be doing well. Interpol data for 1994 showed that 39 per cent of crime in Ireland resulted in a detection, compared with 21 per cent in Denmark, 26 per cent in England and Wales and 30 per cent in Sweden.[38] By 1997 the Irish detection rate had climbed to 43 per cent, while in England

Figure 2: Index of Indictable Crime, 1990–1999
*(1990 = 100)*

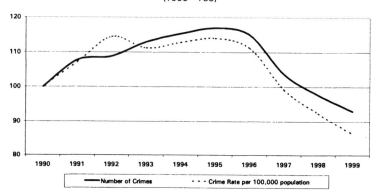

*Source*: Garda Síochána Annual Reports and CSO Population Estimates

Figure 3: Official Detection Rate (%), 1960–1999

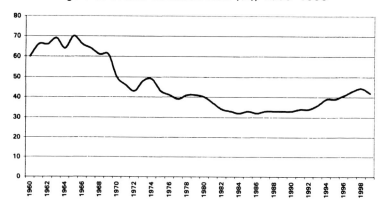

*Source*: Garda Síochána Annual Reports

and Wales it remained static at 26 per cent. In 1999, 42 per cent of indictable crimes were detected. By definition, all non-indictable crimes are detected as they are only recorded if proceedings are brought.

Not all detected indictable crime results in the instigation of criminal proceedings. Between January and September 1999, no proceedings were shown in one in four crimes recorded as 'detected'. If these cases are excluded the detection rate falls from 42 to 33 per cent. Over the past ten years, the gap between the official detection rate and the number of detected cases in which proceedings were commenced has grown. As shown in Figure 4, the detection rate is less impressive if limited to cases where proceedings are taken. It would seem that there are also some detected cases in which proceedings are taken, but that do not result in a conviction. If these were excluded, the detection rate would fall slightly further. It would aid in the interpretation of Garda statistics if the definition of what constituted a detected crime was spelt out clearly.

The detection rate may be higher in Ireland because the Garda Síochána is more efficient and effective than its counterparts in other countries. Or it may be that reported offences are handled differently here. If the latter, it is not clear how much comfort can be drawn from an increasing detection rate.

The very rapid rate of increase in crime from the 1960s was not unique to Ireland. Virtually all industrialised countries showed significant increases in crime in the period following the Second World War.[39] This was despite 'massive rises in living standards, expenditure on the criminal justice system and

**Figure 4: Detection Rate for Indictable Crime, 1990–1999**
*(percentage)*

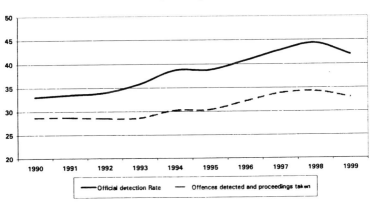

*Source:* Garda Síochána Annual Reports

Figure 5: Crimes Recorded by the Police, Percentage Change, 1988–1998

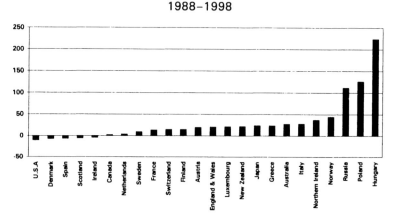

*Source*: C. Gordon, G.C. Barclay and C. Tavares, *International Comparisons of Criminal Justice Statistics 1998,* (London: Home Office, 2000)

measures of personal security' in such countries.[40] Between 1988 and 1998, in countries for which data are available, only a small number, of which Ireland was one, showed a decrease in crime, as Figure 5 illustrates.

The countries with the largest increases in crime were the post-communist countries of Russia, Poland and Hungary, with other countries showing more modest rates of change. While the substantial increase in crime in the post-communist states is largely attributable to their transition from command to market economies, explaining the reasons why some countries have experienced a decrease in crime is more problematic.[41]

One key factor that must be taken into account in understanding cross-national variations in crime rates is the priority different societies place on different forms of behaviour. Sweden, perhaps surprisingly, has the highest crime rate in Europe. Table 2 provides a breakdown of recorded crime for 1990 and 1998. It shows that serious crimes are relatively rare, but fraud, driving while intoxicated, tax offences and bicycle theft are taken seriously and constitute a major part of the official crime statistics. In Ireland, these offences rarely appear in the Garda figures.

TABLE 2: Crimes Reported to the Police in Sweden

|  | 1990 | 1998 |
|---|---|---|
| Accessory to another's death | 350 | 157 |
| Offences against the occupational safety law | 328 | 183 |
| Murder or manslaughter and assault leading to death | 121 | 187 |
| Environmental offences | 486 | 324 |
| Rape, incl. aggravated | 1,410 | 1,998 |
| Tax offences | 6,331 | 6,444 |
| Robbery, incl. aggravated | 5,967 | 6,793 |
| Driving while intoxicated | 25,508 | 12,495 |
| Burglary | 22,446 | 17,645 |
| Drug offences | 26,517 | 32,534 |
| Fraud | 106,699 | 43,522 |
| Assault, incl. aggravated | 40,690 | 58,264 |
| Auto theft | 51,064 | 48,251 |
| Shoplifting | 64,533 | 63,109 |
| Bicycle theft | 106,672 | 102,848 |
| Destruction of property | 96,963 | 120,889 |
| Other offences or theft | 485,160 | 484,489 |
| Total offences | 1,218,820 | 1,193,378 |

*Source*: Government of Sweden, *Sweden in Figures 2000*. (Örebro: Sweden,

As Figure 6 shows, Ireland has a comparatively low crime rate with 2,311 recorded crimes per 100,000 population, only slightly ahead of Japan, Russia and Spain, with New Zealand and Sweden recording the highest number of crimes per 100,000 population.

Figure 6: Crimes per 100,000 Population, 1998

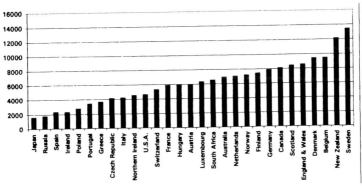

*Source*: C. Gordon, G.C. Barclay and C. Tavares, *International Comparisons of Criminal Justice Statistics 1998*, (London: Home Office, 2000)

Interestingly, when we examine the prison population per 1,000 recorded crimes (Figure 7), we obtain almost a direct reversal of the pattern. Sweden and New Zealand are towards the bottom of the league, whereas Russia, Spain, Japan and Ireland are clustered together towards the top. In other words, despite having relatively low rates of crime, the aforementioned countries resort extensively to imprisonment, whereas the Nordic countries, despite having high official crime rates, use imprisonment spar-

**Figure 7: Prison Population per 1,000 Recorded Crimes, 1998**

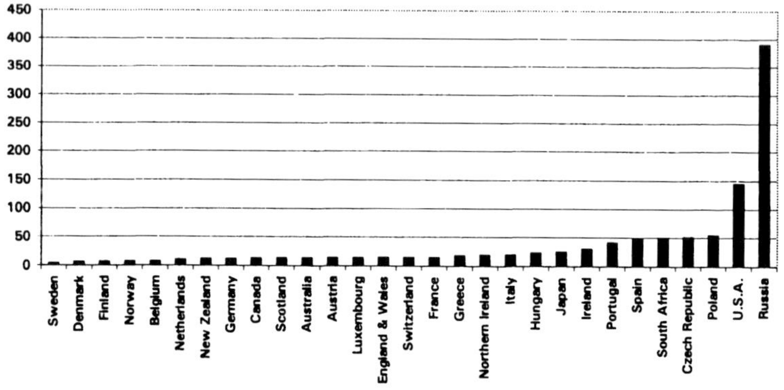

Source: C. Gordon, G.C. Barclay and C. Tavares, *International Comparisons of Criminal Justice Statistics 1998,* (London: Home Office, 2000)

ingly.

Despite the fall in crime, expenditure on both the Garda and the prison service has risen rapidly over the past decade as is shown in Table 3. An estimated £200m has been set aside for prisons in 2000 and a staggering £672m has been earmarked for the Garda.[42]

In Table 4, we have calculated the cost of each recorded indictable crime in Ireland since 1990. On the basis of these calculations, based on current prices, each indictable crime will soon cost in excess of £8,000. In 1997 it was £5,300, while the equivalent figure for England and Wales in the same year was stg£1,500.[43]

TABLE 3: Expenditure on the Garda and Prison Service,
1990–1999

|      | Expenditure on Prisons £m | at constant 1990 prices | Expenditure on Gardaí £m | at constant 1990 prices |
|------|------|------|------|------|
| 1990 | 78  | 78  | 298 | 298 |
| 1991 | 85  | 82  | 315 | 305 |
| 1992 | 92  | 86  | 341 | 319 |
| 1993 | 96  | 88  | 377 | 347 |
| 1994 | 105 | 94  | 391 | 350 |
| 1995 | 108 | 94  | 406 | 352 |
| 1996 | 121 | 103 | 440 | 374 |
| 1997 | 152 | 126 | 479 | 399 |
| 1998 | 189 | 152 | 569 | 457 |
| 1999 | 189 | 148 | 580 | 455 |

*Source*: Department of Justice, Equality and Law Reform Accounts Branch and Estimates for Public Services, various years

TABLE 4: Cost of Crime

|      | No. of In-dictable Crimes (,000) | Expenditure on Garda (£m) | Expenditure per Crime (,000) | at constant 1990 prices (,000) |
|------|------|------|------|------|
| 1990 | 87.7  | £298 | £3.4 | £3.4 |
| 1991 | 94.4  | £315 | £3.3 | £3.2 |
| 1992 | 95.4  | £341 | £3.6 | £3.4 |
| 1993 | 99.0  | £377 | £3.8 | £3.5 |
| 1994 | 101.0 | £391 | £3.9 | £3.5 |
| 1995 | 102.5 | £406 | £4.0 | £3.5 |
| 1996 | 100.8 | £440 | £4.4 | £3.7 |
| 1997 | 90.9  | £479 | £5.3 | £4.4 |
| 1998 | 85.6  | £569 | £6.7 | £5.4 |
| 1999 | 81.3  | £580 | £7.1 | £5.5 |

*Source*: An Garda Síochána and Department of Justice, Equality and Law Reform

## Official Crime Categories

Total indictable crime figures, although telling us something about the increase or decrease in crime generally, are not particularly helpful in discerning trends in particular types of crime. The Garda Annual Reports divide indictable crime into four categories.

- Group I (offences against the person) are generally seen as the most serious crimes. Murder, assault, wounding and sexual crimes are included in this category.

- Group II (offences against property) is the next most serious category. This group includes burglary, robbery, making and causing explosions and unlawful seizure of vehicles.
- Group III (larcenies) includes larceny from the person and of motor vehicles, and fraud.
- Group IV (other) contains a range of miscellaneous offences such as treason, indecent exposure, public mischief and conspiracy.

On average, Group II and Group III offences together have accounted for over 95 per cent of all reported and recorded indictable crime in Ireland since the 1960s. Group III (other larcenies) alone accounts for nearly 60 per cent of all indictable crime each year. Group I offences typically account for two per cent of the total. Thus, when crime increases, the bulk of this is accounted for by less serious crime. An index of crimes in each group is shown in Figure 8. It clearly shows that since 1995 significant decreases have occurred in Group II and Group III offences, but that Group I offences have actually increased in frequency.

Figure 8: Index of Indictable Crime by Category, 1990–1998
*(1990 = 100)*

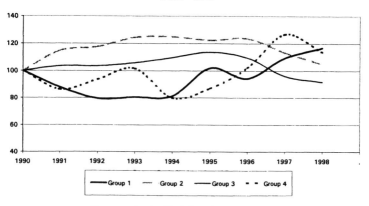

*Source*: Garda Síochána Annual Reports

While Group I offences have shown an increase over the past five years, much of this is as a consequence of the increased number of sexual crimes (Figure 9).

Figure 9: Sexual Crime in Ireland, 1990–1998

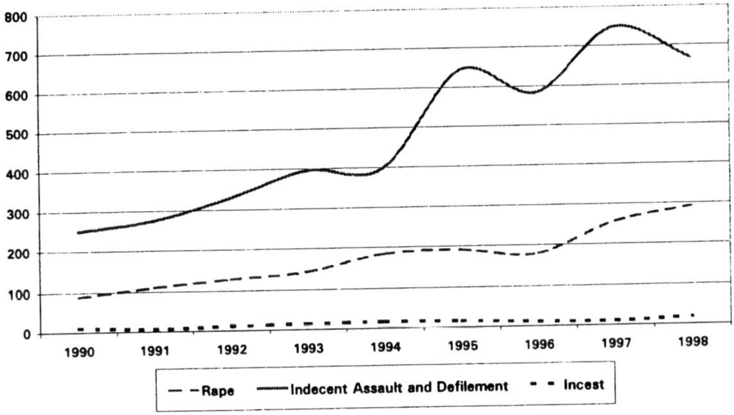

Source: Garda Síochána Annual Reports

In 1980, 46 rapes were recorded by the Garda. By 1990 this had almost doubled to 89, and by 1999 it had trebled again to 278. To some extent this reflects a growing willingness on the part of victims to complain, even about incidents which may have taken place many years previously.[44] Despite this, the number of rapes known to the Garda is comparatively low, as can be seen in Table 5.

TABLE 5: Number of Rapes per 1,000
Population, 1997

| | |
|---|---|
| Greece | 0.2 |
| Switzerland | 0.5 |
| Portugal | 0.6 |
| **Ireland** | **0.7** |
| Germany | 0.8 |
| Denmark | 0.8 |
| Finland | 0.9 |
| England & Wales | 1.3 |
| Scotland | 1.4 |
| Sweden | 1.5 |
| Belgium | 1.7 |
| Northern Ireland | 1.8 |
| Australia | 7.7 |
| South Africa | 12.1 |

Source: Sixth Survey on Crime Trends and the Operations of Criminal Justice Systems, (United Nations, 2000)

Similarly, while the number of murders has increased in recent years, the overall numbers are still low by international standards, as Table 6 highlights.[45] High homicide countries, as Elliot Currie points out, are characterised by widespread availability of firearms and extremes of economic inequality and material deprivation.[46]

TABLE 6: Number of Homicides per 1,000
Population, 1998

| | |
|---|---|
| Norway | 0.86 |
| Denmark | 0.93 |
| Luxembourg | 0.94 |
| Austria | 0.95 |
| Switzerland | 1.07 |
| Japan | 1.10 |
| Germany | 1.19 |
| **Ireland** | **1.41** |
| England & Wales | 1.43 |
| Portugal | 1.52 |
| Netherlands | 1.57 |
| Italy | 1.60 |
| France | 1.64 |
| New Zealand | 1.68 |
| Australia | 1.78 |
| Canada | 1.83 |
| Greece | 1.93 |
| Scotland | 1.95 |
| Poland | 1.96 |
| Sweden | 2.11 |
| Belgium | 2.14 |
| Finland | 2.19 |
| Spain | 2.61 |
| Hungary | 2.85 |
| Czech Republic | 3.04 |
| Northern Ireland | 4.44 |
| U.S.A. | 6.26 |
| Russia | 20.20 |
| South Africa | 57.52 |

*Source:* C. Gordon, G.C. Barclay and C. Tavares, *International Comparisons of Criminal Justice Statistics 1998,* (London: Home Office, 2000)

Also of note is that nearly 60 per cent of all recorded indictable crime is in Dublin, but when broken down by category of offence, just over 30 per cent of Group I offences took place in the capital, compared with in excess of 60 per cent of larcenies. The highest rate of crime per head of population is usually recorded in Dublin North Central (139 per 1,000 in 1999). The lowest rates are usually in found in Mayo and Roscommon/ Galway East (per 1,000 in 1999).

Although the majority of murders occur in Dublin (22 out of 38 in 1999), as Figure 10 shows, it remains a relatively safe city in international terms.

Figure 10: Average Annual Homicides per 100,000 Population, 1996–1998

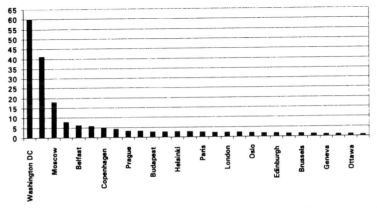

Source: C. Gordon, G.C. Barclay and C. Tavares, *International Comparisons of Criminal Justice Statistics 1998,* (London: Home Office, 2000)

Comparatively few crimes of 'fraud' are recorded by the Gardaí as shown in Table 7. The phrase 'white collar crime' is often associated with scandals in the financial and business world and the sophisticated frauds of senior executives. It is related to what is popularly known as corporate crime, which includes the many activities of powerful corporations which exploit relatively powerless consumers, workers and citizens. Some criminologists have argued that these kinds of crime are more widespread, more serious, and more damaging to society than many other common crimes such as robbery or burglary. In our view, ignoring the crimes of the wealthy is a dangerous bias.

Hazel Croall put it well when she wrote that

> white collar crime is not generally regarded as part of
> the 'crime problem'. The public tend to be far more
> afraid of being mugged, raped or robbed by a stranger
> on the street than they are of being killed on a
> commuter train, poisoned at a wedding party or
> seduced by a host of misleading advertisements, cheap
> bargain offers or bogus investment schemes.[47]

TABLE 7: Fraud in Ireland, 1999

|  | No. known offences | Criminal proceedings commenced |
|---|---|---|
| Embezzlement | 38 | 9 |
| Other fraud | 115 | 80 |
| Fraud by agents/trustees | 6 | 3 |
| Fraud by bogus advertisers | 0 | 0 |
| Fraud by bogus sales persons | 2 | 0 |
| Fraud by bogus companies | 0 | 0 |
| Fraud by obtaining credit | 20 | 13 |
| Fraudulent conversion | 14 | 8 |
| Falsification of accounts | 1 | 1 |
| **Percentage of total crime** | **0.3** | |

*Source:* Garda Síochána Annual Report, 1999 (Jan.–Sept. incl.)

Others, however, have argued that conventional street crime is a threat to the ability of a society to sustain meaningful community life, a threat which is not posed by white collar crime. Public order is not violated in business offences as it is in conventional crime and such offences have a much less threatening character. It may be true that a business practice such as tax evasion is not as threatening as physical assault, but crime such as pollution, the mass marketing of defective drugs or the deliberate neglect of safety standards pose real dangers to a great number of people.

Despite this, white collar crime is not generally regarded as part of the crime problem. This illustrates the notion that crime itself is socially constructed and that white collar crimes are not readily defined as crime.[48]

It is difficult to write with any confidence about the extent of corporate crime in Ireland. The official statistics give few clues. For example, according to the most recent Garda statistics, there were no known cases of fraud by a company in 1999. In his book about the sociology of crime in Ireland Ciaran McCullagh outlined how the criminal justice system 'criminalises the offences of young working-class men and systematically ignores the crimes of the middle class'.[49] He described the extent and nature of corporate fraud, tax evasion and insider dealing and argued persuasively that the spotlight of critical inquiry should be brought to bear on those involved in the crimes carried out in corporate suites as well as on corporation streets. In the four years since McCullagh's book appeared, unprecedented attention has been focused on tax evasion by banks and their customers, payments to politicians and corruption in the planning process.[50] However, at the time of writing (September 2000), no person has been convicted of any of these activities in a criminal court.

Figure 11 shows the trend in non-indictable crime since 1960. Like indictable crime, there was a steep overall decline after the early 1980s. This was followed by some years of fluctuation and a sustained reduction since the mid-1990s. As we argue later,

**Figure 11: Non-Indictable Crime – Proceedings Taken 1960 1999**

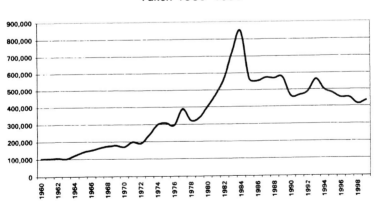

*Source*: Garda Síochána Annual Reports

this overall decrease conceals some worrying increases in certain categories of non-indictable crime.

In summary, the existing official data suggest that we have witnessed a very large increase in the number of indictable crimes recorded by the Garda since the late 1960s. The bulk of this is accounted for by the increase in crime against property, rather than against the person. As crime rates increased, the detection rate decreased, but in recent years it has risen again. A disproportionate number of crimes against property are committed in Dublin. Since 1995, the overall rate of indictable crime has decreased. Non-indictable crime has also decreased over the past number of years.

## The Accuracy of Official Statistics

There are considerable difficulties in taking the official rate of crime at face value. Criminal statistics are famously imperfect. [51] As Leon Radzinowicz, one of the founding fathers of British criminology, remarked in 1945, they are 'difficult to compile, difficult to comprehend, and difficult to interpret'.[52] The passage of time has not eased these difficulties.

National and local crime surveys and self report studies have been utilised to uncover the 'dark figure of crime', i.e. the volume of criminal activity that goes unreported by the public or unrecorded by the police. Victimisation surveys focus on the extent to which individuals experienced crime, but for various reasons did not report it to the police. This does not necessarily mean that such surveys provide a more accurate picture of the extent of crime, rather that they provide a different perspective. As Maguire argues, such surveys give 'an alternative, rather than a directly comparable overall picture of crime to that offered by police statistics: it is "fuller" than the latter in some respects, but "narrower" in others'.[53] One particular limitation of household victimisation surveys is that they exclude persons of no fixed abode and those in institutions. These groups may have atypical experiences of crime.

## The 'Dark Figure' of Crime

There are a few examples of victim surveys in the Irish literature and they indicate that the official data considerably underestimate the level of crime,[54] but to an extent this discrepancy is broadly in line with other countries.[55]

The most recent was conducted as part of the Quarterly National Household Survey carried out by the Central Statistics Office (CSO) in September–November 1998.[56] A total of 39,000 respondents were asked about crimes against themselves or their households which had taken place during the previous twelve months. The data generated through these interviews provide a valuable point of contrast with the Garda statistics.

Figure 12 shows that very few motor vehicle thefts (five per cent) were not reported.[57] This can be explained by the requirement to notify the Garda if an insurance claim is to be made. However the Garda statistics indicate that only about one in three of these reports was officially recorded. It would seem that more than 10,500 have disappeared from the books. With respect to burglaries, one-third of the incidents which victims say they reported do not appear in the official crime statistics. This amounts to 15,000 missing burglaries. For theft from motor

Figure 12: Unreported and Unrecorded Crime, 1998

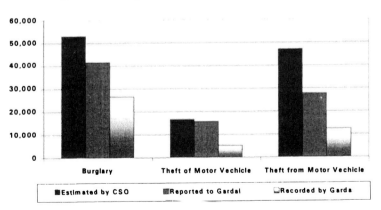

*Source*: Garda Síochána Annual Reports

vehicles, more than half of all reports (15,400) that victims say they made do not appear to have been recorded.

In other words it would seem that the Garda statistics under-represent the level of crime and that in reality there are twice as many burglaries, three times as many thefts of cars and four times as many thefts from cars. It is important to identify the factors which might explain the dark figure.

## Why Not Report Crime?

According to the CSO survey the most common reasons for not reporting crimes were that the offence was not serious enough or a belief that the Garda could not, or would not, do anything. However, we know nothing about why crimes are not recorded by the Garda. It may be that incidents which respondents considered burglary, for example, would be defined (and recorded) otherwise by gardaí, or that victims' recall was faulty, or that for a variety of valid operational reasons certain allegations did not become part of the official record. It may also be that offences which were unlikely to be detected were omitted.[58] This latter explanation would go some way towards explaining why the detection rate is so high. As noted earlier, in 1999 it stood at 42 per cent compared with 33 per cent ten years earlier. It is time that this seemingly simple statistic was subjected to scrutiny. It may reflect differential recording rather than investigative excellence, but in the absence of research it is not possible to come to any definitive conclusion.

Victimisation surveys are carried out routinely in other countries to provide an alternative source of information to the official statistics. Their value lies in their stability over time. They may reveal that victimisation is increasing despite falls in the official rates, or *vice versa*. Official crime statistics can be affected dramatically by changes in recording practice which are independent of changes in criminal victimisation. It is to be hoped that the CSO victimisation survey will be continued on a biennial basis, as its real value will only be revealed through repetition.

One survey can only show up the disjuncture between recorded crime and victimisation rates. Surveys repeated at regular intervals are required if we are to learn anything about trends.

The decision whether or not to record an incident as a crime depends on the extent to which the police are prepared to deal with the matter formally. Once again we know little about the dynamics of this process in Ireland, except that as the CSO survey showed there is under-recording on a vast scale. There are some excellent examples in the British literature of how the police respond to allegations of serious crimes, such as assault and rape, and how the interplay of victim attitude, offender characteristics and police priorities all contribute to the decision to take formal action.[59]

Rather than treating the rate of indictable crime as the actual extent of crime in any given year, it is better viewed as an index of crime. Because of the apparent stability in the manner in which indictable crime figures are collated and categorised by the Garda, it can be argued that the data presented in Figure 1 above are indicative of general trends in the extent of crime.

## Fear of Crime

The CSO survey also contained useful information about risk of victimisation and fear of crime. Men aged 18–24 years were most vulnerable to theft or assault, with risk declining by age. However, they did not feel fearful. Elderly women were a low risk group but reported feeling unsafe. The proportion that felt crime was 'a very serious problem in Ireland today' was higher for women in every age group and increased with age for both men and women (see Figure 13). At a time when there are significant reductions in crime rates, it is a matter of concern that people are so anxious.[60] This finding is supported by a survey of public attitudes to crime in 1999, which showed that 89 per cent of interviewees believed crime was on the increase.[61]

Victimisation studies conducted in other countries show a similar pattern: we know that the typical victim is, in fact, very much like the typical criminal – not old, female and wealthy, but male, young, single, a heavy drinker and involved in assaulting others – and that the fear of crime is greater than the reality.[62] The mismatch between fear of crime and risk of victimisation may be explained by the lack of accurate public information about crime rates, a political debate which is mired in the rhetoric of 'zero tolerance', and media distortion.

Figure 13: How do you Describe Crime in Ireland Today?

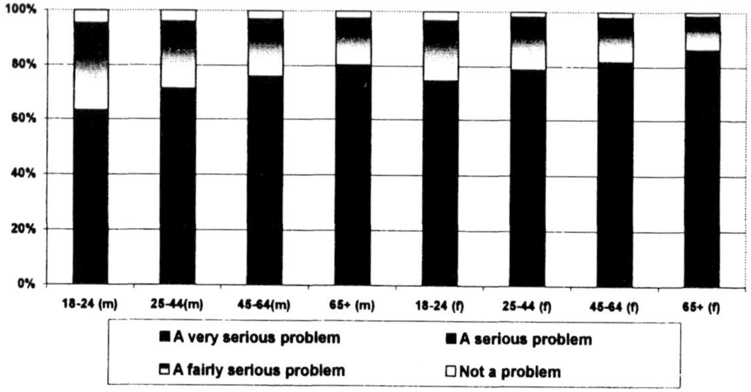

*Source*: Central Statistics Office, *Quarterly National Household Survey – Crime and Victimisation 1998* (Dublin: CSO, 1999)

The CSO survey also asked how safe people felt walking in their neighbourhood and whether they felt safe alone in their home at night. Over 70 per cent said that they felt very safe or safe walking in their neighourhood at night and over 90 per cent felt safe or very safe at home at night. In a similar pattern to perceptions of fear of crime (as shown in Figure 14), as people got older, particularly women, they felt less safe.

Crime is a minor risk in most people's lives. Research suggests that the public is likely to exaggerate the frequency of rare, serious crimes and underestimate the frequency of more common, less serious ones.[63] In the real world crimes occur in inverse proportion to their seriousness; the more serious the crime, the more rarely it occurs. One key source of the distortion in people's perceptions is the mass media.

Figure 14: Perceptions of Crime and Safety by Age and Gender (%)

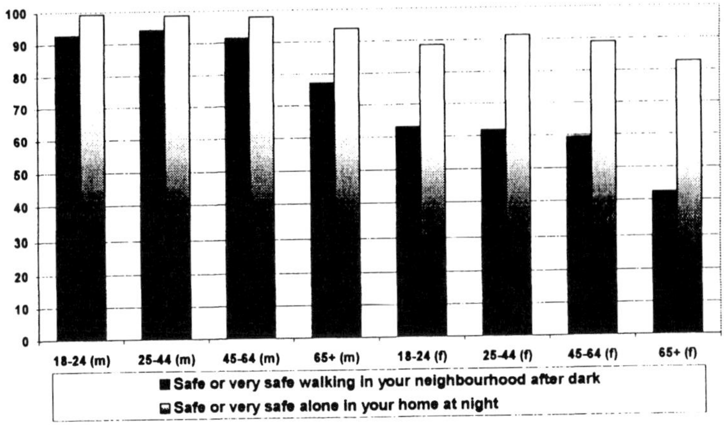
100
90
80
70
60
50
40
30
20
10
0
18-24 (m)
25-44 (m)
45-64 (m)
65+ (m)
18-24 (f)
25-44 (f)
45-64 (f)
65+ (f)
Safe or very safe walking in your neighbourhood after dark
Safe or very safe alone in your home at night

*Source*: Central Statistics Office, *Quarterly National Household Survey – Crime and Victimisation* (Dublin: CSO, 1999)

## Crime and the Media

In a series of articles, O'Connell and his colleagues argued that no relationship existed between official statistics and the public estimate of crime prevalence.[64] They investigated whether rates of victimisation affected perceptions of crime, but found they did not. In a detailed multi-variate analysis of newspaper readership, they suggested that, controlling for class and education, those who regularly read Independent Group newspapers (*Irish Independent* and *Evening Herald*) had the highest or most pessimistic view of crime prevalence. Their research concluded that there is a disproportionate number of crime stories dealing with extreme and violent offences; comparing crime stories that appear in the press, greater newsworthiness is given to more serious and extreme offences; crime stories highlight vulnerable victims and invulnerable offenders and general articles about crime are pessimistic. This argument echoed an analysis by Gene Kerrigan and Helen Shaw in 1985 that editorial executives in the Independent Newspaper Group adopted a policy designed to change the presentation of this issue (the level of crime against readers) from one of 'a manageable problem into a crisis'.[65]

At the beginning of the twenty-first century, Ireland has a comparatively low rate of crime and one that is decreasing, although it is uncertain how long this will remain the case in light of the fact that a similar decrease occurred in the early 1980s and was followed by a sustained increase. Recorded crime in the main is against property rather than against the person. This is not to dispute that certain property crimes (such as residential burglary) can have traumatic consequences. Despite this, as we argue in the following sections, the politics of criminal justice in Ireland has become more punitive, increasingly targeting the poor, while largely ignoring the crimes of the wealthy.

## 3. The Origins of 'Zero Tolerance' Irish Style

In the early part of the 1990s a new approach to crime began to emerge from the Department of Justice. For the first time a concerted attempt was made to think strategically about criminal justice issues and to publish detailed policy statements. The first discussion document to be generated by this process – *The Management of Offenders: A Five-Year Plan* – appeared in June 1994 during Maire Geoghegan Quinn's tenure as Fianna Fáil Minister for Justice. The Minister described it as 'the first major policy document published by the Department'.[66]

*The Management of Offenders* reviewed progress towards the implementation of the recommendations made nine years earlier by the Whitaker Committee of Inquiry into the Penal System and set out a time frame for their final implementation.[67] At the heart of the five-year plan was a realisation that prison should be used to the minimum extent compatible with the need for public safety. This view was driven by an awareness of the enormous costs associated with depriving people of their liberty. The plan recommended constructing an additional 210 prison places and setting an upper limit of between 2,200 and 2,300 on the number of prisoners. To allow this would involve significant investment in programmed early release and the provision of an adequate range of non-custodial penalties.

When the government changed in December 1994, the five-year plan was shelved. The rainbow coalition's Minister for Justice, Nora Owen, set to work on a much more detailed overview of the criminal justice system and the challenges facing it. The product of this review – *Tackling Crime: A Discussion Paper* – was published in May 1997, and like her predecessor the Minister introduced it as 'the first ever document of its kind'.[68]

*Tackling Crime* was a thoughtful and wide-ranging report. It attempted to fashion a set of criminal justice policies fit for the twenty-first century by setting out twelve goals for the Department of Justice:

- Fostering research and providing quality information
- Inter-agency cooperation
- Continuous review of the criminal law
- Efficient and cost-effective use of Gardaí resources
- Dealing with substance abuse (including alcohol) and 'organised' crime
- Providing an effective system of legal aid
- Ensuring the operation of the courts is speedy, fair and value for money
- Creating an accountable prison service
- Developing a system of alternatives to custody
- Providing a forum for debate on crime and punishment
- Supporting victims
- Ensuring sufficient resources are available to carry out these functions

A general election was declared within a week of the publication of this document. Six weeks later, Nora Owen's nemesis, John O'Donoghue, was installed as Minister for Justice (with added responsibility for Equality and Law Reform). To all intents and purposes the *Tackling Crime* document disappeared from political discourse with the change of government. It may, of course, have continued to influence the thinking of key civil servants.

Between the publication of the *Management of Offenders* and *Tackling Crime,* the tenor of the debate about crime and punishment had undergone a dramatic shift. The murders of Veronica Guerin and Jerry McCabe in June 1996 gave rise to a massive growth in law and order rhetoric. In the twelve months between these killings and the general election of June 1997, Fianna Fáil redefined itself as the party of law and order.

The architect of this redefinition was its justice spokesperson since 1995, the Kerry solicitor John O'Donoghue, who was a pivotal force in the politicisation of law and order. He painted a disturbing picture of a country under threat, a place where extreme measures were required if the centre was to hold:

> The task of the next government will be to use the human and physical resources in this country to confront the malaise of crime and to foster, in the Ireland of the twenty-first century, an environment in which the traditional Irish values of community, compassion and caring can flourish. That task will not be easy. It is not a task amenable to glib or shallow solutions. But it is a task which cannot be shirked or circumvented. The social fabric of this country is being destroyed. The next government must wage war on the cause of that destruction. It must wage war on crime. It must wage war on the causes of crime – the social causes, the economic causes, the educational causes. Each must be identified, isolated and eradicated. This is the challenge which faces the next government.[69]

When Fianna Fáil returned to government after the election, O'Donoghue took over the Justice brief and began to wage his war. Criminal justice policy had previously been an area of public life where inertia and disinterest were occasionally punctured by crises and bouts of hysteria.[70] When these crises had been averted or managed, interest was soon lost. Policy making was one of many functions carried out by a small and overburdened Department of Justice. However, John O'Donoghue changed all this. He made law and order into a central part of political life by accentuating the differences between Fianna Fáil's hardline policies and what he portrayed as the ineffectual approach of the Government parties.

It was an impressive achievement for the Department of Justice to produce a document as measured as *Tackling Crime* at a time when Fianna Fáil in opposition was taking every opportunity to talk up the problem of crime. It was by no means inevitable that the killings of Veronica Guerin and Jerry McCabe would result in a significant and enduring 'punitive shift' in criminal justice policy. It is clear that even in the immediate aftermath of these deaths, the Department of Justice was working steadily on the production of *Tackling Crime*. The change in the political tempo was created by Fianna Fáil in opposition and maintained by them in government. The introduction of 'zero tolerance' became something of a personal crusade for O'Donoghue when he took the reins in the newly expanded Department of Justice, Equality and Law Reform.

In November 1996, within months of the Guerin and McCabe killings, and supposedly at the height of public concern about law and order, there was a referendum to widen the grounds on which bail could be refused. There was almost universal political support for the change. If the public were as agitated about crime as the politicians thought, they would have been rushing out in droves to remove this important safeguard. In the event there was a very low turn-out: 580,000 people voted yes, 195,000 voted no, and 1,880,000 did not bother to vote at all.[71] In other words one in five registered electors voted to amend the Constitution. By the time the Bail Act 1997 eventually came into force in full (15 May 2000), whatever public and political anxiety existed in 1996 appeared to have evaporated.

There are clear precedents for horrific killings sparking public horror and outrage which in turn lead to massive policy and legislative shifts and are translated into surges in police activity, prison populations and so on. This is not a uniquely Irish phenomenon. A case in point is the record rise in the prison population in England and Wales following the killing of James Bulger, the infant dragged to his death on a railway line by two ten-year-old friends (see Figure 15).

Figure 15: Prison Population England and Wales, 1990–1999

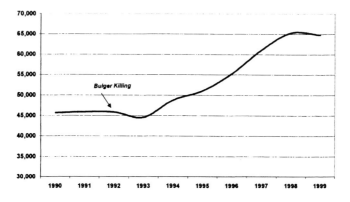

*Source*: C. Cullen and M. Minchin, *The Prison Population in 1999: A Statistical Review* (London: Home Office, 2000)

The number of prisoners in England and Wales had been dropping steadily in the months leading up to this killing. An innovative new piece of legislation (the Criminal Justice Act 1991) had just come into force and greater use was being made of non-custodial penalties. The 1991 Act was the result of exhaustive consultation and was greeted as a watershed in criminal justice policy. However, it was facing opposition from magistrates who felt their discretion to punish was being interfered with, and from some sections of the media.[72] James Bulger's killing changed the nature of the debate in a matter of days. Attitudes hardened. Politicians ratcheted up the stakes. Angry crowds gathered outside the courts to taunt, abuse and try to injure the two children who had taunted, abused and mortally injured another child. The Prime Minister of the day (John Major) called for more condemnation and less understanding. The Home Secretary (Michael Howard) declared that prison worked.

The terminology is different in Ireland, but the political sentiment is identical. Instead of steering public opinion towards moderation at a time of crisis, politicians seized the opportunity to further inflame passions.

According to Robert Reiner, Professor of Criminology at the London School of Economics, horrific crimes such as the killing of James Bulger become 'occasions for orgies of punitiveness and anguished Jeremiads about moral decline'.[73] He suggests that crime control policy and discourse takes place on two levels – pragmatic approaches based on risk reduction for the more mundane offences, and moral panics about the exceptional crimes of violence. Responses to the latter ('orgies of punitiveness') serve to assuage popular anxiety and frustration symbolically, whilst the former are geared to provide as much routine protection as is possible and affordable.

## 'Zero Tolerance' Policing

In March 1997, Fianna Fáil, then in opposition, published a document entitled *Leading the Fight Against Crime,* derided at the time by Vincent Browne as 'devoid of fact, analysis, costings or reflection'.[74] Two of its key proposals were the promise of an additional 2,000 prison places and the introduction of a policy of 'zero tolerance'.

'Zero tolerance' is a shorthand term for criminal justice policies that are based on the principles that no crime is insignificant or will be overlooked and that tolerance of small crimes creates a climate in which big crimes flourish. This link between disorder, fear of crime, and more serious crime, is associated with the work of James Q. Wilson and George L. Kelling from the United States, who proposed the 'broken windows' theory to explain it.[75] This theory proposes that if a window in a building is left unrepaired the other windows will soon be broken. They further suggested that 'untended' behaviour also leads to the breakdown of community controls. If a house is left abandoned and untended, for example, the weeds will grow, a window may be smashed, children are allowed to be noisy, litter accumulates, young people congregate, public drinking and begging occur and there are fights.

This breakdown need not lead inevitably to increases in more serious crime. But Wilson and Kelling proposed that the change in the neighbourhood will affect residents' perceptions of crime. The level of disorder will lead them to assume that crime, especially violent crime, is rising. This will make them feel less secure and more fearful. They will change their behaviour, using the streets less often and avoiding contact with others. This will weaken community bonds and increase individual isolation. Such circumstances make an area more vulnerable to crime, according to Wilson and Kelling. It is more likely, though not inevitable, they say, that drug-dealing, prostitution and muggings will visibly flourish there, more so than in a place where people are confident in the informal controls of public behaviour. [76]

This idea is appealing at a time when people are sick and tired of crime, feel overwhelmed by its apparently relentless upward trend and want firm action taken against, for example, drunken loutish behaviour, intimidating gatherings of young people in public areas, the public use of obscene language, aggressive begging, litter, graffiti, drug-dealing and prostitution.[77] There are, however, considerable difficulties in defining what constitutes disorder and whose definition of disorder achieves priority.[78]

What exactly is meant by 'zero tolerance' policing is in itself contested. The phrase was originally associated with feminist groups campaigning against male violence inflicted on women and children. Launched in Edinburgh in November 1992 as an initiative by the City Council's Women's Committee, the Zero Tolerance Campaign was developed as a public education strategy which sought to raise awareness about the extent and nature of male violence against women and children, to send out a clear message that such crimes should not be tolerated, and to call for a national strategy to combat male violence. In

1997, the European Parliament called on the European Commission to undertake research into violence against women in the European Union and promote Edinburgh District Council's 'zero tolerance' campaign on a European basis.[79]

Other advocates of 'zero tolerance' policies, in addition to claiming concern about serious crime, also tend to believe that the quality of life is being eroded, that society is becoming less civilised and that drastic measures are required to restore order. This version of 'zero tolerance' has little to do with crime, rather it represents a particular worldview of the present, laced with nostalgic perceptions of the past. As Pearson argues, this 'juxtaposition of lawless modernity as against the stable traditions of the past, which uses the past as a stick to beat the present, is a vital political metaphor in the contemporary world'.[80]

Thus, two quite distinct interpretations of 'zero tolerance' have been advanced. One developed by feminists is historically aware, recognising the long history of violence against women and children and aiming to ensure such actions should not be tolerated in the future. The other perspective is historically naive, fearful of the present and seeking to return to a golden age of civility, a past that, certainly in Ireland, we are slowly becoming aware concealed a wide range of criminal activities.

The perspective adopted by Fianna Fáil is intolerant of non-conformity and fearful of change. To restore certainty, civility and stability, the police and other agencies must exercise the full range of their coercive powers. Those members of society whose behaviour upsets and threatens need to be rendered docile and to conform to elite perceptions of appropriate conduct. Irish society, in the summer of 1996, was increasingly perturbed by the apparent growth in crime and this was exploited by Fianna Fáil in the lead-up to the general election in 1997. 'Zero tolerance' effaces the distinction between the mundane offences, which are 'managed' according to Reiner, and the serious offences, which unleash naked hunger for retribution. It creates a climate which is risk averse and promotes harshness *especially* for less serious offences.

This concept of 'zero tolerance' was borrowed from New York, where it had been used by the Republican mayor, Rudolph Giuliani, and put into action by police chief William Bratton.[81] Both men forged new careers on their crime fighting credentials.[82] As Bratton put it:

> New Yorkers wanted a way out of the danger and lawlessness they saw around them. They couldn't walk from their apartments to the subway without being accosted by an aggressive beggar or threatened or worse. They couldn't walk to work without seeing men and women using the streets as outdoor toilets. They couldn't stop their car at a traffic light without some guy smearing their windshield with a filthy rag and demanding a dollar. Squeegee men, these fellows were called, and it seemed they just about ruled the city. I had joked that they should replace the torch in the Statue of Liberty's hand with a squeegee. New York felt like a city under siege and nobody was doing anything about it.[83]

The election of Rudolph Giuliani as Mayor of New York City in 1993 and the appointment of William Bratton as Police Commissioner in January 1994 ushered in a period of vigorous organisational 're-engineering' in the New York Police Department (NYPD). The key elements of their new model were as follows:

- The NYPD and its officers were provided with clear crime reduction objectives, such as 'get guns off the streets', 'curb youth violence in the schools and on the streets', 'drive drug dealers out of New York' and 'break the cycle of domestic violence'.
- Information systems were substantially improved to provide police managers with up-to-date data on crime 'hot spots' and weekly trends down to the local level. Previously this information had only been available on a quarterly basis and at a relatively high level of aggregation.
- Precinct commanders were made accountable for crime in their areas and, more particularly, for developing and implementing focused local crime reduction strategies.

- Weekly planning sessions of senior management and precinct commanders, known as 'Compstat' meetings, were introduced. These sessions utilised crime-mapping techniques to highlight crime hot spots, plan the allocation of resources, and actively monitor the performance of local commanders.
- Police were encouraged to use strict enforcement of minor offences where appropriate as a means of disrupting patterns of criminal activity and discouraging the carrying of firearms. Other frequently utilised strategies included: saturating areas with uniformed or plainclothes officers; setting up checkpoints to find stolen cars; conducting vertical patrols in buildings; using nuisance abatement laws to shut down illegal businesses; and undertaking sting operations and narcotics 'buy and bust' operations.
- Local commanders were empowered to deploy detectives and specialised units to assist in tackling crime problems in designated areas, rather than these units operating to their own individual objectives as had traditionally been the case.[84]

Bratton took his fight against crime to the streets. He energised a jaded and demoralised police department and restored his officers' belief that they could control their precincts. There were co-ordinated crackdowns on minor public order offences such as public urination, drunkenness, begging, and fare evasion on the subway. In some cases people arrested for such crimes were found to have outstanding warrants against them, to be in violation of the conditions of their parole, or in possession of drugs, knives or guns. By concentrating on so-called petty offenders, serious criminals were also captured and offensive weapons were taken out of circulation. Behaviour which had previously been considered anti-social rather than criminal was tackled aggressively. Lawlessness, no matter how minor, was to be stamped out.

As noted above, central to Bratton's strategy was the use of Comprehensive Computer Statistics (Compstat) and the holding of local precinct commanders to account.[85] Numbers were crunched and scrutinised at regular meetings. Commanders had to know what was going on in their areas in minute detail. They had to demonstrate their motivation, performance and willingness to be held to account. They had to justify their entitlement to remain in post. Underachievers were shown the door. During Bratton's brief reign, three-quarters of New York's precinct commanders were changed. Compstat was the engine behind 'zero tolerance'. In essence this was data-driven policing underpinned by slick public relations and a supportive media.[86]

Bratton began his term as Police Commissioner in January 1994. His promise was to reduce crime by 40 per cent in three years. He said when he was appointed that he would take the city back for the people who lived there, neighbourhood by neighbourhood, block by block, house by house: 'We were going to fix the broken windows and prevent anyone from breaking them again.'[87]

On the face of it his approach appears to have met with resounding success. The annual number of murders in New York peaked at 2,262 in 1990 and dropped to 767 in 1997. Between 1993 and 1996 the homicide figures fell by 50 per cent.

However, the fall in crime cannot be explained by different police practices alone.[88] There were a number of other contributory factors such as demographic changes (an ageing and therefore less crime-prone population), a massive rise in the prison population, substantial increases in police strength, and the waning of the 'crack' cocaine epidemic that had been the cause of so much crime.[89] Furthermore, the NYPD had for some time been operating below an effective level – corruption was widespread and police were not engaged with the business of policing. To some extent the force began doing what it should have been doing anyway.

New management techniques and structures of accountability certainly helped to depress crime rates, but it is difficult to disentangle their contribution relative to wider social trends. A steep decline was already well advanced *before* Bratton took the reins, and it continued after his departure.[90]

It is important to remember that 'zero tolerance' principles can quite easily veer into an oppressive style of policing which is against, rather than with, the community. Christian Parenti has described it as 'the science of kicking ass'.[91] While undoubtedly popular with right-wing politicians and intuitively appealing to uninformed electorates, it is crucial to remember that 'zero tolerance' can only be effective with a community's consent and active participation. The targets of 'zero tolerance' are typically disenfranchised urban males, living at the margins of society. The consequences of singling out identifiable groups or areas for heavy-handed policing are well documented. [92] When the targets of this policing are from minority groups the conditions are in place for widespread disruption, such as the rioting in Brixton in south London in 1981 which resulted from the behaviour of (white) police officers towards the (black) local community, and the aftermath of the beating of black motorist Rodney King by a group of white police officers in Los Angeles in March 1991.[93]

What is acceptable in New York may not be in Dublin. There would be little stomach in Ireland for an absolutist policy of 'zero tolerance'. Tactics that work in a densely populated multi-ethnic city, with a high homicide rate, a huge 'underclass' and an armed police force may not translate well into other contexts. In addition, and crucially, the link between disorder and serious crime has not been established conclusively: less nuisance does not guarantee less serious violence. In other words, the key foundation of the 'zero tolerance' philosophy is shaky.

Interestingly, Bratton denied that what he did in New York was to implement a policy of 'zero tolerance'. Indeed, he rejected the term as simplistic and misleading. He believed that, taken to its logical conclusion, 'zero tolerance' meant a blanket end to police discretion and this would be impossible to implement in a modern disorderly society. As he put it: 'It is not a credible policy: it communicates to political leaders and the general public an unrealistic view of what we can accomplish

. . . 'Zero tolerance' is neither a phrase that I use nor one that captures the meaning of what happened in New York City, either in the subways or on the streets.'[94]

'Zero tolerance' denies the complexity of police work and the exercise of discretion by officers. It is a hollow slogan. No police department has the wherewithal to enforce all of the laws all of the time. Depending on local circumstances and resources, police will use their discretionary powers to enforce the law differentially.

In Ireland, no less a figure than the Garda Commissioner, Pat Byrne, expressed reservations about this new way of policing as soon as it was proposed. He proclaimed himself 'very sceptical' about Fianna Fáil's idea of 'zero tolerance' as expressed in *Leading the Fight Against Crime.* He said that if a government was to tell him to initiate 'zero tolerance' policing, he would have to respond: 'Exactly what do you mean?' The Fianna Fáil justice spokesperson, John O'Donoghue, pounced on the Commissioner: 'Perhaps the Commissioner would assist the debate by following through on his public criticism of Fianna Fáil's "zero tolerance" policing policy by stating the categories of crime and the levels of crime which he believes to be tolerable.'[95]

Despite concerns about what is really meant by 'zero tolerance', exaggerated claims of its effectiveness, and the danger of it veering into an oppressive form of policing, Fianna Fáil developed an infatuation with the idea. New York-style policing came to Ireland through the offices of Bratton's deputy, John Timoney. Timoney, a native of Dublin, emigrated to the United States at the age of thirteen. After graduating from high school, he joined the New York Police Department. His early years in the Department were on the streets of New York, first as a patrol officer and then as a narcotics specialist. In 1980, he was promoted to sergeant and began a meteoric rise through the ranks which culminated in his appointment in 1994 as the youngest Chief of Department in the history of the NYPD. A year later, Timoney was named as First Deputy Commissioner, second in command of the NYPD. In this capacity, he oversaw a major reorganisation of the Department, including its merger with the New York Transit and Housing Police Departments to create a unified city police department. He retired from the NYPD in 1996, beginning a new career as a consultant and adviser on policing to local and national governments and police agencies around the world, including membership of the Steering Group established to review the efficiency and effectiveness of the Garda.[96] He is now the Police Commissioner of the City of Philadelphia.

Timoney helped Fianna Fáil to draw up its 'zero tolerance' approach to crime before it returned to government in June 1997.[97] His influence shines out of the Fianna Fáil election manifesto for 1997:

> Fianna Fáil will make a broadly-based war on crime a central priority of our first years in government. Our strategy is to fight each and every crime through effective law enforcement, while at the same time attacking the root causes of crime that arise through social deprivation.
>
> Crime in Ireland has become dramatically worse. So-called 'petty crime' has mushroomed. We have seen an alarming growth in serious violent crime, most of it drugs-related. Organised crime has suddenly emerged as a vicious reality in Irish society. Crime threatens us on our streets, in our homes and in our businesses.
>
> Fianna Fáil in government will:
>
> Develop a long-term national crime strategy
> Adopt a zero tolerance policy on all crime
> Strengthen the Garda, increasing the force by 1,200
> Speed up courts procedures and set up a Prisons Authority
> Expand prison places by 2,000.

A parallel development took place in Britain.[98] In 1996 both Michael Howard (Home Secretary) and Jack Straw (Shadow Home Secretary) visited New York and came back impressed by what Bratton had achieved. This new approach to policing became an issue in the 1997 general election. In September of that year, Jack

Straw, by now Home Secretary himself, announced in a speech to the Labour Party conference that he wanted 'zero tolerance of crime and disorder in our neighbourhoods'.

Fianna Fáil returned to power after the 1997 general election. Its share of the vote was 39 per cent, exactly the same as in the 1992 general election,[99] when the concept of 'zero tolerance' had not existed. The fact that the party gained nine seats and returned to government was more to do with tactical vote management and the collapse of support for the Labour Party than the public's desire for new law and order policies. Its return to government depended on coalition with the Progressive Democrats (who had also adocated a 'zero tolerance' policing policy) and the support of four independent deputies. Fianna Fáil was not returned on a swelling of public support for the politics of 'zero tolerance'. Fine Gael, whose crime policies were more measured and moderate, also gained nine seats in the 1997 election.

John O'Donoghue, who had been so bullish in opposition as Fianna Fáil Justice spokesman, was given the portfolio he had shadowed so aggressively. In her welcome to the new government, former Minister, Nora Owen, described the effect of John O'Donoghue's numerous scathing attacks on her when he was in opposition: 'I am now battered and bruised with welts and scars from the two and a half years I spent in the Department of Justice.' She was harsh in her condemnation of the tactics used against her by the opposition:

> The House should turn its back on sloganising which gets in the way of real debate. Prior to the election we witnessed the meaninglessness of what Fianna Fáil referred to as zero tolerance . . . That gets in the way of serious debate. The Minister for Justice, Deputy O'Donoghue, will be watched carefully by me and others on the opposition benches in view of all he said as Opposition spokesperson on Justice. I promise he will have a difficult time. It is time we dealt with the crime issue in a more unilateral and non-divisive manner. There was much divisiveness and headline-grabbing in the past two-and-a-half years with some

Members saying, 'I am tougher than you.' That is not good enough and is not the way to get answers to our crime problem. The outgoing government adopted multi-faceted policies. It is not enough just to build prisons and introduce tough legislation.[100]

After its return to government, Fianna Fáil's commitment to 'zero tolerance' never wavered. Despite the rapidly changing social and economic context, and a declining crime rate, John O'Donoghue stuck rigidly to his election promises. The public would get more prisons, more gardaí and less tolerance, no matter what.

O'Donoghue has certainly lived up to his promises. When he took up office the allocation provided in the 1997 Estimates for the Garda Vote was a figure of £479m. The provision in the Estimates for the year 2000 is £672m, an increase of 42 per cent. The overall Department of Justice, Equality and Law Reform budget increased from £698m under the last administration to £1 billion in 2000, a 43 per cent increase. The strength of the Garda increased from a base of 10,800 to 11,458 in August 2000, and is expected to reach the planned level of 12,000 by the year 2002.[101]

An important policy document was published by the Department of Justice, Equality and Law Reform in 1998. This was a three-year strategic plan called *Community Security and Equality* and it built on the foundations laid in *Tackling Crime*.[102] The plan set out the broad direction for the Department until the end of the year 2000. It highlighted 79 objectives cutting across the entire spectrum of criminal justice activities and outlined both the strategies that would be put in place to realise these objectives and appropriate output measures.

Two of these objectives were concerned with 'zero tolerance' policing. Objective 4 stated: 'Maintain the zero tolerance policy momentum against substance abuse and serious crime, including so-called "organised" crime'. Objective 12 was: 'Pursue a zero tolerance approach towards crime, including white collar crime'. Interestingly, this objective had no associated strategy or output measures. Even more interestingly, neither objective was included in the evaluation of the Garda policing plan in 1999.[103] Furthermore, 'zero tolerance' does not feature in the Garda corporate strategy for 2000–2004.

When he opened the National Crime Forum on 26 February 1998, the Minister emphasised that he was as resolute as ever:

> Nothing which I have seen or experienced as Minister for Justice, Equality and Law Reform has in any way altered my view that a policy of 'zero tolerance' towards crime is the only effective policy. A total war on crime is, and will remain, the goal of this government. For so long as crime remains a major social problem it is the duty of the government to do everything within its power to eradicate crime.[104]

# 4. Explanations of Crime Trends

## The Traditional Critique

Some commentators have identified the crime rate as a barometer of social change. Increases in crime are attributed to the growth in 'permissiveness' and the more general disintegration of society as we know it. Such a perspective was articulated by the then Garda Commissioner, Patrick Culligan, in an *Irish Times* article in September 1994, a time when the crime rate was heading for an all-time peak.[105]

Culligan portrayed a society in transition in which traditional authorities were being challenged, new social norms were evolving and more opportunities to offend were becoming available. He outlined eight key transformations that in his view had led to the increase in crime. They were:

- dismantling the authority of the family
- closing reformatory and industrial schools
- outpatient care for the mentally ill
- prison sentences being reduced inordinately by an unpredictable temporary release system

- social pressure for both parents to go into the labour force
- dismantling teachers' authority
- abandonment of the religious ethic
- dispersal of established communities from city centre locations to new housing schemes many miles away

The social trends highlighted by Commissioner Culligan were all apparent in 1994 and in the following years they intensified. This should have led to an escalation in crime.

If by dismantling the authority of the family he meant the decline of the traditional nuclear family, he was correct, and this trend has accelerated since his article was published. According to the 1996 census, there has been a 15 per cent increase in the number of lone-parent households with children in the state, from 109,600 in 1991 to 125,500 in 1996, with more than four in five of them headed by women. Almost 72 per cent of lone-parent households were in urban areas. In more than 45 per cent of lone-parent families in 1996 a widowed person was the parent. In a further 28 per cent the lone parent was separated, while single parents accounted for 15 per cent. There were more than twice as many broken marriages in 1996 than ten years previously. The increase in the number of separated people (including divorced couples) between 1986 and 1996 was 136 per cent. There were 87,800 separated (including divorced) people in 1996, compared with 55,100 in 1991 and 37,200 in 1986. The Census report shows that the greatest growth occurred in the categories 'legally separated' and 'other separated', each of which more than doubled between 1991 and 1996. Deserted women outnumbered men by 10,000 (16,785 compared with 6,363).

Industrial and reformatory schools have been closed since the early 1970s. Yet it is hard to square the closure of these schools with an increase in crime. If anything, in some cases, such institutions created very damaged individuals some of whom later committed crime, and a considerable number of people committed criminal acts while working in these schools.[106] Certainly, the view of probably the most notorious criminal in recent Irish history, Martin Cahill, was that 'if anyone corrupted [him] it was those mad monks down in the bog'[107] – a reference to the Oblate fathers who ran the Daingain Reformatory.

The number of psychiatric patients cared for in the community has increased and the number cared for in traditional institutional settings has decreased. The number of public psychiatric inpatient beds, excluding beds for the elderly and for mentally handicapped patients, fell from 12,416 in 1982 (5.32 per 1,000 adult population) to 5,055 in 1996 (1.96 per 1,000).[108] As with the industrial and reformatory schools, it is difficult to determine a correlation between the introduction of more humane standards of psychiatric care and rates of offending. Nor is there a clear relationship between mental illness and criminality.

In recent years Temporary Release (TR) has been used much less frequently as a safety valve to cope with prison overcrowding. The prison-building programme has eased the pressure on accommodation in the crowded committal prisons (especially Mountjoy). It has slowed down the 'revolving door'. This has led to a substantial reduction in the number of prisoners serving their sentences outside the prison walls. Of 3,228 prisoners in custody on 12 July 2000, 219 were on temporary release (seven per cent). This compares with 506 prisoners on temporary release out of a total of 2,730 prisoners (19 per cent) on 10 July 1996.[109]

In the 25 years between 1971 and 1996, women's employment grew by 212,000, reaching 488,000 in 1996 according to labour force surveys. This shift particularly involved married women, with only 38,300 employed in 1971 compared to 203,000 by 1996. Participation rates based on the International Labour Organisation classification of employment and unemployment show even greater increases. On this classification, 507,700 women were in employment in 1996 and 41 per cent of Irish women aged 15 and over were active in the labour force.[110] The surge in female employment has continued in recent years. In 1998 female participation rates increased to 44 per cent; by May 1999 they had reached the EU average of 46 per cent and by August 1999 they had risen to 50 per cent.

Culligan noted that teachers' authority has declined in Ireland. Perhaps by this he meant that teachers are unable to impose the same discipline on pupils as they did in the past. Certainly a key aspect of control in Irish schools, corporal punishment, was formally abolished in 1982, but again it is difficult to reconcile the abolition of a cruel and degrading practice with an increase in crime.

If by religious ethic, Culligan meant a decline in vocations and attendance at mass, he was correct on both points. Vocations declined from 608 in 1980 to 91 in 1999,[111] and in urban areas attendance at mass has dropped very significantly. A 1998 Prime Time survey indicated a national average of 60 per cent, but the figure was as low as six per cent in some working-class Dublin parishes.

Local authorities continue to build on greenfield sites on the outskirts of urban centres, albeit not on the same scale as they did during the 1970s. Such estates are often portrayed as having considerable crime problems, but recent research has highlighted their heterogeneity.[112] In addition, some established city centre communities often had a well-established history of criminal activity prior to dispersal.[113]

In other words, the trends that Culligan identified as contributing to the increase in crime in Ireland exist in even more exaggerated form today, with the exception of high levels of TR, yet recorded crime has decreased substantially. The traditional explanation appears to be of little analytical value. Can anything be learned then from comparative analyses of social change?

## A Nation not Obsessed with Crime?

In an interesting book published in 1983, Freda Adler examined the factors that characterised ten countries with low crime rates.[114] Ireland was included in her selection along with Switzerland (both Western European countries), Bulgaria and the German Democratic Republic (European Socialist countries),

Costa Rica and Peru (Latin American), Algeria and Saudi Arabia (Islamic countries in North Africa and the Middle East), Japan and Nepal (Pacific and Asia).

Adler looked at the relationship between 47 socio-economic and demographic indicators and arrest rates. Low-crime countries were compared with the average for other countries in their region. One interesting finding was that seven of the ten low-crime countries had fewer telephones per 1,000 population than the mean number for their respective regions. Perhaps this made crime reports less likely? However, the same was true for a sample of high-crime rate countries (8 of 11 had fewer telephones per 1,000 than the average for their region). She concluded, 'It is clear from the statistical analyses presented here that the available "hard" data produced little in the way of meaningful information on the relationships between socio-economic and cultural indicators and crime rates.'[115]

These disappointing findings resulted in a change of emphasis to an examination of less formal mechanisms of social control. This allowed the identification of some (tentative) commonalties. Low-crime countries shared criminal justice systems that were popular and seen as legitimate, and strong social controls that existed outside the criminal justice system (specifically family and religion). These were 'capable of maintaining, generating and transmitting shared values'.[116] The loosening of the ties that bind in family, community and church created an environment where the brakes on crime were released.[117]

Based on opinion poll data, confidence in the Garda has generally been high.[118] Recent detailed research by the Economic and Social Research Institute (ESRI) indicated that while over 80 per cent of individual victims were satisfied with their initial contact with the Garda, only one-third were satisfied with the information made available to them on the progress of their case and only one-quarter were satisfied with the information made available on its outcome.[119] The levels of satisfaction with the service provided by gardaí are a cause for concern. As the ESRI interviewees were likely to be favourably disposed towards the

Garda in that they did not decline to participate in the study when contacted by the Garda Research Unit, it is likely that overall levels of dissatisfaction are higher than reported here. Only one in five of this pre-selected group believed that the Garda did a 'very good' job controlling crime.[120] The least positive ratings came from victims of the most serious offences (assault and aggravated burglary).

It seems clear that the conditions identified as protective by Adler no longer exist. This should lead to crime rates soaring. However, they are not. As all the 'obvious' correlates of crime increase, the crime rate decreases. We must look elsewhere for a convincing explanation.

## Crime and Modernisation in Ireland

Some commentators have associated the growth in crime with the modernisation of Ireland.[121] The most sophisticated of these analyses have been made by McCullagh, for whom the underlying causes of crime are located in the double marginalisation produced by the process of economic and social development over the past 30 years.[122] This is the marginalisation of significant sectors of the working class from the benefits of development, and the marginalisation of sectors of the middle class from regulation generally and from the legal system specifically. His theory aims to explain: rising amounts of crime since the 1960s; the co-existence of property crime committed by young working-class males and the occupational and corporate crime committed by middle-class men; the low participation rates of women; the degree to which crimes of violence have remained relatively low; and the extent to which crime is urban- and particularly Dublin-based.[123]

McCullagh emphasises that he is advancing an argument which draws on and utilises available empirical data but which has not itself been the subject of empirical investigation. He argues that 'dependent development' in Ireland has influenced crime in four ways.[124] Firstly, new levels of affluence led to new opportunities for crime. Secondly, the weakness of the State in regulating multi-national corporations led to white collar crime. Thirdly, it undermined the traditional sources of employment that the working classes were dependent on and replaced them with new kinds of employment that were rural-based and for which few had either the education or the requisite skills. Fourthly, such marginalisation was not as intense for working-class women, and other social roles were available to them.

Official reports have also tended to implicitly draw on modernisation theory to interpret crime in Ireland. For example, the Report of the Inter-Departmental Group on Urban Crime and Disorder, which was established by the government following serious public order incidents in one area in Dublin, rather than attempting to explain the causes of crime in Ireland, instead identified criminogenic areas, which it argued would typically have the following characteristics:

- a large, predominantly single-class housing estate, built in the past twenty years or so with very few amenities, e.g. local shops, access to professional services, playgrounds;
- a relatively young parent group, with an above-average number of dependants but with very few older family connections (such as grandparents) residing nearby;
- above-average unemployment levels, with some experiencing long-term (and 'second generation') unemployment and with many residents in quite poor financial circumstances;
- a small percentage of the adult population having second- or third-level educational qualifications;
- a higher than average tendency towards criminal and anti-social behaviour.[125]

While these various explanations assist us to a degree in interpreting the rapid growth in crime in Ireland from the mid-1960s, they are less convincing in explaining the rapid decrease in crime in recent years (or indeed in the mid-1980s). Based on these accounts, the crime rate in Ireland should be increasing rather than decreasing. Could it be that the explanation lies in the criminal justice policies introduced by John O'Donoghue as Minister for Justice, Equality and Law Reform?

A press statement issued by the Department of Justice, Equality and Law Reform in August 2000 is full of self-congratulation:

> There is no question but that the Minister's policies are working. The number of crimes reported to the Garda Síochána in each of the three years since he took up office has declined and is tangible proof of the success of his anti-crime measures . . . [There has been] a staggering drop of 21 per cent in reported crime since this government took office.

In the next section we examine the development of current criminal justice policies and explore the possibility that a shift in political emphasis has led to the decline in recorded crime. Has crime fallen due to 'zero tolerance' and more prison places?

## The Role of the Police in Constructing Crime Rates

Socio-legal work carried out in other jurisdictions gives some clues about the extent to which the police 'construct' a suspect population.[126] We know nothing about how members of An Garda Síochána exercise their discretion on a day-to-day basis, and to what extent the decision to arrest and charge someone is a matter of case-by-case negotiation.[127] David Rottman analysed the fate of those who were arrested by gardaí in Dublin in 1981.[128] Only half of all these arrests resulted in prosecutions. Clearly there are many instances where gardaí decide not to pursue matters. Unfortunately we have no knowledge of how these decisions are made.

Nor do we have any systematic understanding of 'cop culture'. A substantial literature exists in other countries that tries to explain police activity, which is sometimes manifestly discriminatory, with reference to the existence of a powerful and constraining occupational culture.[129] Reiner has gone so far as to state that police powers, 'are primarily directed against the young, male, disproportionately black, economically marginal, street population which threatens the tranquillity of public space as defined by dominant groups'.[130] One wonders to what extent this generalisation would hold true in Ireland, perhaps (so far) with the exception of the racial dimension.

Some small insights can be gleaned from the statistics contained in the annual reports of An Garda Síochána, particularly if one looks at those offences where Garda initiative is more pronounced. One example of how gardaí may use their discretion to criminalise the economically marginal is the continued use of the Vagrancy Acts, under which begging remains illegal, in that 'any person wandering abroad and begging or placing himself in any public place, street, highway, court, or passage to beg or gather alms, or causing or procuring or encouraging any child or children to do so shall be liable on conviction to imprisonment for a period not exceeding one month'.[131] This statute – enacted to control the desperate poor when the famine was at its height – is still in force today.

'Zero tolerance' is really about the non-indictable, so-called quality-of-life crimes. As we argued above, the basic premiss of this approach is that 'serious street crime flourishes in areas in which disorderly behaviour goes unchecked'.[132] If it was working there would be a massive rise in summary offences, especially as these are often the offences which the police generate directly rather than ones which are reported to them by victims. In other words, changes in policing would be quickly reflected in a different pattern of certain categories of non-indictable crime.

## Beggars

Vigorous prosecution of beggars would be an example of 'zero tolerance' in practice. 'Street people' have been the focus of concerted 'zero tolerance' police tactics in other countries, where they are moved on, picked up and shipped out.

In the Law Reform Commission's *Report on Vagrancy* it was stated that the annual number of prosecutions for begging had fallen from an average of 424 in the 1960s to 303 in the 1970s.[133] The annual number of prosecutions continued to fall until the mid-1990s. Between 1990 and 1996 proceedings against beggars were initiated on an average of 128 occasions each year. Since 1997 and the official call for 'zero tolerance' policing, proceedings have rapidly increased, as is shown in Figure 16. The average number of prosecutions each year between 1997 and 1999 was 508.

Figure 16: Zero Tolerance 1: Criminal Proceedings
Taken against Beggars

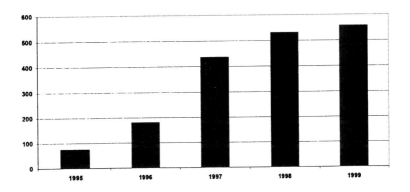

*Source*: An Garda Síochána Annual Reports

It is a cause of some concern that the criminal law is used at all to penalise poverty and social inadequacy. This is hardly the hallmark of an enlightened society. The notion that beggars might be more vigorously pursued is abhorrent. The contrast with the lack of energy devoted to the pursuit of white collar criminals could not be more marked. As Jonathan Swift observed: 'Laws are like cobwebs, which may catch small flies but let wasps and hornets break through.'[134]

At a time of unparalleled economic prosperity the continuing prosecution of the visible, and in some ways troubling, poor is a sobering reminder that economic poverty remains entrenched. The fact that there has been a significant rise in arrests and prosecutions of beggars is evidence that 'zero tolerance' rhetoric has real life consequences. The prosecution of begging is one example of how the Garda Síochána plays a role in generating the official picture of crime.

## The Disorderly

What about other categories of 'nuisance crime'? Gearoid Carey views the Criminal Justice (Public Order) Act 1994 as opening the way for serious unfairness and discrimination, as gardaí single out for attention those categories of society they believe need to be controlled. 'Targeting is the epitome of the rule of discretion, arbitrariness, stereotype and uncertainty, and consequently such practices involve the antithesis of the rule of law.'[135] It can be seen from Figure 17 that since the introduction of the Act there has been a marked, and sustained, increase in the number of proceedings taken against those who are perceived as offending against public order. The Act criminalises, for example, intoxication in a public place (section 4), disorderly conduct in a public place (s. 5), threatening or abusive or insulting behaviour (s. 6) and failing to comply with the direction of a garda (s. 8).

Figure 17: Zero Tolerance 2: Criminal Proceedings Taken under the Criminal Justice (Public Order) Act 1994

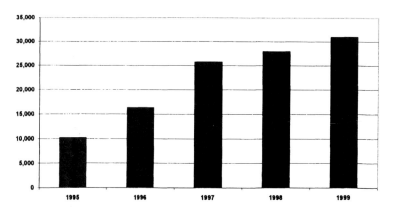

*Source*: Garda Síochána Annual Reports

## Prostitutes

Soliciting or importuning for prostitution, and loitering with intention of prostitution are other classic cases of crimes which enter the statistics only in the event of direct action by the Garda. They are defined by sections 7 and 8 of the Criminal Law (Sexual Offences) Act 1993. Arrests rarely result from 'victim' complaints. Once again, if one looks carefully at the statistics for non-indictable crime, a worrying trend emerges, as is shown in Figure 18. The average number of prosecutions in the two years prior to the 1997 general election was 60, compared with 650 in the following two years.

**Figure 18: Zero Tolerance 3: Criminal Proceedings Taken under the Criminal Law (Sexual Offences) Act 1993**

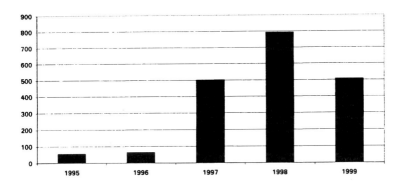

*Source*: Garda Síochána Annual Reports

It would seem that the overall reduction in crime conceals a number of interesting trends. While indictable crimes have declined, there has been an increase in offences against the person (Group I offences). Similarly, while the volume of non-indictable crime has declined, there have been increases in proceedings taken against the very types of offender who would be targeted by 'zero tolerance' policing.

It may be that the increase in proceedings against beggars reflects an increase in the level of homelessness. Between 1996 and 1999, the numbers of officially recorded homeless persons more than doubled from 2,501 to 5,234.[136] However, an increase in the number of people living, drinking, drug-taking, begging and soliciting on the street should not necessarily lead to an increase in the use of the criminal law against these individuals. Social policy rather than criminal justice policy offers a more constructive and humane mechanism to meet the needs of these vulnerable groups.[137]

We are not suggesting that John O'Donoghue has attempted to influence the operation of Garda powers or the exercise of their discretion. There does not have to be a direct link between the Minister, Commissioner and gardaí on the beat. What we hope to demonstrate is that a climate of 'zero tolerance' can permeate all levels of society and may influence the nature of some aspects of policing, even if the Garda Síochána has never formally embraced the philosophy of 'zero tolerance'.

No one would doubt that firm measures are required to deal with serious crime. Increasing the risk of arrest and the certainty (and sometimes severity) of punishment must be key elements of any criminal justice policy. The problem with 'zero tolerance' is that it singles out for special attention the very group already subject to surveillance and targeting – namely the visible offenders (beggars, public drunks and abusive young men). These groups may constitute a public nuisance, but they are not responsible for many of the serious crimes that affect society. Killings, violence and sexual abuse often take place within the family home and are not preventable by the aggressive policing of public space. Fraud, theft and other white collar and corporate crimes may be planned in financial centres, exclusive restaurants and on golf courses. Again, they are hardly amenable to the politics of 'zero tolerance' as expressed through high visibility policing.

'Zero tolerance' predicts that an emphasis on tackling quality-of-life crimes (begging, prostitution, street disorder etc.) will have the knock-on effect of reducing serious crime. The pattern observed in Ireland is precisely the opposite of this. A more intense focus on nuisance offences has not brought down the rate of violent crime. Beggars and public order offenders in Dublin are unlikely to be carrying guns (as they sometimes were in New York) or to be on the run from a police force in a different state. It is difficult to learn anything from the official statistics, or from increased prosecution of the marginalised, about why crime rates are declining.

## Does More Prison Means Less Crime?

Perhaps the crime rate is going down because of the government's extensive prison-building programme. There can be little doubt that the incapacitative effect of imprisonment exercises some downward pressure on crime rates. However, the extent of this effect is often exaggerated. In probably the best attempt to quantify this association, Roger Tarling came up with the following broad rule of thumb: an increase of 25 per cent in a country's prison population will reduce the rate of recorded crime by one per cent.[138] In other words, prison has a marginal effect on crime rates. Tarling's analysis ignores crimes committed within prisons and the criminogenic consequences of imprisonment.

Policies that place too much reliance on prison are unlikely to achieve much in terms of public protection. Looking at the increasing use of prison in Ireland (Figure 19), it can be said that if Tarling's rule holds true then the 32 per cent increase in the average daily prison population between 1997 (2,227) and 1999 (2,929) is likely to have resulted in just over a 1.2 per cent reduction in the crime rate. However, the crime rate declined by 10 per cent over this period, suggesting that other, more significant factors were at play, in addition to a slight incapacitative effect.

The increased prison population may be due to a greater through-put of prisoners or an increase in average sentence length. Unfortunately it is impossible to disentangle the relative importance of these factors as the most up-to-date detailed prison statistics available at time of writing relate to 1994.

Figure 19: Daily Average Custody in Irish Prisons, 1960–1999

*Source*: Annual Reports on Prisons and Places of Detention

The swelling prison population may also be a result of the increase in crimes against the person, which is often lost sight of in the excitement about the overall reduction in recorded crime. These more serious offences attract heavy penalties and if the perpetrators are appearing in court with greater regularity, there will be an obvious effect on the size of the prison population. Recent figures show that the number of murder and rape cases returned for trial at the Central Criminal Court rose from 58 in 1993 to 157 in 1998, and the number of cases returned for trial at the Dublin Circuit Criminal Court rose from 873 to 1,132 over the same period.[139]

Two other countries, Greece and South Africa, have shown a larger increase than Ireland in their imprisonment rate between 1997 and 1999 (Table 8). One factor that accounts for the increase in prison populations in Europe that has not yet significantly affected Ireland is the increasing rate of incarceration of 'foreign prisoners', usually asylum seekers. In 1997, 39 per cent of the Greek prison population were 'foreigners', and 32 per cent in the case of the Netherlands.[140] In South Africa, the rapid increase is attributed to the expansion in the number of unsentenced prisoners, a result of changing sentencing policies.[141] In the case of Ireland these factors do not apply.

TABLE 8: Imprisonment Rate: Prisoners per
100,000 Population

|  | 1997 | 1999 | % change |
|---|---|---|---|
| Greece | 55 | 70 | 27 |
| South Africa | 320 | 400 | 25 |
| **Ireland** | **65** | **80** | **23** |
| Australia | 95 | 110 | 16 |
| Norway | 55 | 60 | 9 |
| Russia | 685 | 730 | 7 |
| Netherlands | 85 | 90 | 6 |
| Germany | 90 | 95 | 6 |
| USA | 645 | 680 | 5 |
| England & Wales | 120 | 125 | 4 |
| Scotland | 119 | 120 | 1 |
| Sweden | 60 | 60 | 0 |
| Japan | 40 | 40 | 0 |
| Canada | 115 | 110 | -4 |
| Finland | 55 | 45 | -18 |
| Northern Ireland | 95 | 70 | -26 |

*Source:* R. Walmsley, *World Prison Population List* (Home Office Research, Development and Statistics Directorate, 2000).

In America, one well known commentator, Charles Murray, has argued that 'zero tolerance' style policies and 'three-strikes and you're out' legislation have contributed to the decline in crime.[142] The massive increase in the use of imprisonment is viewed as of central importance. At the end of June 1999, 1,860,520 persons were incarcerated in America, with a prediction that by the year 2001, in excess of two million Americans will be behind bars.[143] In 1999 this represented a rate of incarceration of one in every 147 US residents. During 1998, 68 prisoners were executed and at the end of 1998 3,452 prisoners were under sentence of death. Between 1988 and 1998 there was an increase of 90 per cent in the number of American prisoners and a ten per cent reduction in crime.[144]

Savelsberg claims that this linkage is more apparent than real, arguing that

While increasing punishment in combination with stabilizing crime rates could be perceived as a rational deterrence response, such an interpretation prompts considerable doubt. First, the steepest and steadiest increase in incarceration rates began in 1980, when the crime rate had already been leveling out during the preceding four years. Second, the incarceration rate increased by more than 50 inmates per 100,000 population between 1980 and 1984 without resulting in any change in the crime rate. In the following years (1984–1989) the incarceration rate grew by an additional 50 again without achieving any change in crime rates. Since 1989 the increase in the incarceration rate has again been 50, as in the two preceding five-year periods, without changing the trend in crime rates but at considerable expense in times of a sluggish economy, declining budgets, and an eroding public infrastructure.[145]

It should also be noted that this increase is not compensated for by a decrease in other forms of punishment, as can be seen in Table 9. Nearly 4.5 million adult men and women were on probation or parole at the end of 1999.[146] This compares to 3.2 million in 1990 and 1.3 million in 1980.

Among the nearly 1.9 million offenders incarcerated on June 30 1999 (as shown in Table 9), more than 560,000 were black males between the ages of 20 and 39. Expressed as a proportion of their representation in the population, 12.3 per cent of black non-Hispanic males aged 25 to 29 were locked up, compared to 4.2 per cent of Hispanic males and about 1.5 per cent of white males in the same age group. Although incarceration rates drop with age, the percentage of black males aged 45 to 54 in prison or jail in 1999 was still nearly 3.4 per cent – twice the highest rate (1.7 per cent) among white males (those aged 30 to 34).[147] Clearly there is a considerable financial and social cost to pursuing a policy of fighting crime with incarceration.[148] By the early 1990s, expenditure on the courts, police and prisons, in the USA was more than double that spent on employment benefits and other employment-related services.[149]

TABLE 9: Correctional Population in the United States, 1980–1999 (,000)

|      | Probation | Jail | Prison | Parole | Total |
|------|-----------|------|--------|--------|-------|
| 1980 | 1,118 | 182 | 320 | 220 | 1,840 |
| 1985 | 1,969 | 255 | 488 | 300 | 3,012 |
| 1990 | 2,670 | 403 | 743 | 531 | 4,348 |
| 1995 | 3,078 | 499 | 1,079 | 679 | 5,335 |
| 1996 | 3,180 | 510 | 1,128 | 680 | 5,483 |
| 1997 | 3,297 | 558 | 1,177 | 695 | 5,726 |
| 1998 | 3,671 | 584 | 1,222 | 696 | 6,124 |
| 1999 | 3,774 | 596 | 1,255 | 713 | 6,289 |

*Source*: Bureau of Justice Statistics *Correctional Surveys* (US Department of Justice, 2000)

More worrying is the view of some observers of the American prison expansion programme, that in light of the number of people behind bars and the concentration of incarceration in the inner-city black population, less coercive institutions of social control such as families or communities may be undermined. The long-term result of this incarceration policy, then, would be increases, rather than the hoped for decreases, in crime.[150]

If the reduction in crime in Ireland is at best marginally related to a massive increase in incarceration or a change in Garda practices, what other factors might explain it? We believe that the answer lies to a large extent in the improved economic situation and other social policy measures.

## Economic, Social and Demographic Factors

As well as examining those areas where the criminal law impacts selectively on the poor, it is possible to look in an aggregate way at the complex and controversial relationship between economic conditions and crime. Generations of criminologists have attempted to unravel the extent to which patterns in crime reflect inequalities in wealth. This has been a rich seam of inquiry. Wolpin's time series analysis of crime rates in England and Wales between 1894 and 1967 showed that the rate of unemployment was positively related to the overall crime rate and specifically to the rate of non-violent property crime.[151] In his trenchant left-wing critique of contemporary criminology, Box argued strongly that long-term unemployment and crime were related, the key intervening variable being the way people interpreted their lack of work, the meaning which it held out to them.[152]

In a thorough review by Chiricos on the crime-employment relationship, it was found that most national level analyses have yielded weak results.[153] Farrington and his colleagues tied crime more directly to employment by examining the timing of crime and employment over almost three years for a sample of teenage males in England.[154] They showed that property crimes were committed more frequently during periods of joblessness. However, this relationship held only for those who were predisposed to crime (as reflected by self-reports on earlier criminal activity and moral values); otherwise spells of joblessness did not induce more offending. More recently, Hale explored the impact on crime of the emergence of a dual labour market – a secondary sector, characterised by part-time, low paid and intermittent employment, existing alongside the primary labour market. He found a long-run relationship between trends in recorded burglary and theft, and the structure of employment.[155]

In terms of methodological sophistication, the work carried out by Simon Field for the English Home Office Research and Planning Unit stands in a class apart.[156] Drawing upon data covering the period 1950–87, he examined the relationship between types of crime and economic variables such as gross domestic product, personal consumption, the level of unemployment, alcohol sales and the number of new cars. By far the strongest relationship was between recorded crime and personal consumption, i.e. the amount spent, on average, by each person in the country in a given year.

There were two main patterns of results. First of all there was a short-term inverse relationship between growth in personal consumption and growth in property crime. In other words, in years when people reduce their spending or increase it very little, property crime tends to grow relatively quickly. In years when people are rapidly increasing their expenditure, property crime tends to grow less rapidly, or even to fall. The explanation lies in the reduced motivation to acquire goods through theft when the capacity to acquire goods lawfully is enhanced.[157] Average increases in consumption are felt most strongly among the poor.

Field demonstrated that this association held throughout the twentieth century in England and Wales. He concluded that 'Economic factors in general, and consumption growth in particular, appear to be among the most important determinants of fluctuations in the growth of property crime in industrialised countries.'[158]

The second significant relationship was between the level of consumption and the rate of personal crime, which was defined to include sexual offences and violence against the person. These factors were positively related: personal crime tended to increase more rapidly during periods of rapidly increasing consumption, and it grew more slowly than usual during periods of slow consumption growth.

Field's explanation was that as consumption increases people modify their routine activities in ways that make it more likely they will become victims of violent crime. For instance, they spend more time outside the home in pubs and clubs, settings where interpersonal confrontations are likely. Indeed, Field found that the growth in beer consumption was the single most important factor in explaining the growth in violent crime. In a survey of 610 incidents of homicide in Ireland over a twenty-year period, it was found that slightly under half of all perpetrators were intoxicated at the time of killing, and in one-third of cases, both perpetrator and victim were affected by alcohol.[159]

Field also found that violence against the person was strongly related to unemployment, particularly long-term unemployment. Thus, as consumption increases, so too does violent crime, but if the consumption growth is accompanied by a fall in unemployment, this dampens down the level of violence.[160]

Field was able to demonstrate a long-run relationship between the economy, demographic factors and recorded burglary and theft.[161] Rapid increases in consumer spending in a given year were associated with falling, or slower growth of, recorded property crime in that year. So there appeared to be a positive relationship between the growth in consumer spending and recorded property crime in the long run, but an inverse relationship in the short run. Field described the former as an 'opportunity effect' (more stealable goods in the economy), and the latter as a 'motivation effect' (when people feel richer, as manifested by their spending, they are less likely to be attracted to criminal methods of obtaining goods). It is not clear why the motivation effect does not endure.[162] Importantly, Field's analysis does not hold true in other countries. A review by the Council of Europe concluded that the strong relationship he identified between crime and the business cycle was peculiar to England and Wales. His findings could not be replicated in other European states.[163]

However, recent crime trends in Ireland – an increase in Group I offences accompanying a substantial reduction in Group II and III offences – demonstrate support for Field's model in the short run. If his analysis applies to the Irish situation, the likelihood is that rates of property crime will increase in the long term. The short-term effect of consumption growth is to hold down crime, but this is balanced by a longer-term reverse effect. In other words, we can expect the current low rate to bounce back.

Figure 20 shows the annual percentage change in GNP per capita in Ireland (a measure of the wealth of the nation), consumer expenditure and crimes of theft and burglary. Here we see a substantial increase in both GNP per capita and consumer expenditure since 1990 and a significant decrease in crimes of theft and burglary. It would seem that there is a strong correlation between increasing consumption, declining male unemployment and the reduction in property crime.[164]

The relationship between crime and demography is a long-standing issue in criminological research. The primary demographic characteristics of age, sex and race are among the

Figure 20: Crime and the Economy 1990–1999 — Annual Percentage Change in Property Crime, GNP per capita and Consumer Expenditure

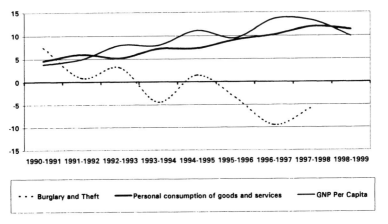

*Source*: Garda Síochána Annual Reports; Central Statistics Office *National Income and Expenditure*, (Dublin: CSO, 1999)

most powerful and robust individual-level risk factors for criminal offending and victimisation. Evidence consistently indicates that young people (particularly between the ages of 15 and 25), males and members of disadvantaged minorities are at comparatively high risk of becoming offenders and victims, at least with respect to the common 'street' crimes. As South and Messner have noted, 'It is hardly an exaggeration to claim that much of the sociological theorising in criminology essentially represents an effort to account for the well-documented "demographic facts" about crime.'[165]

Street crime is a young man's pursuit, regardless of the wider economic situation. An elderly society will have less of the kind of crime that results in a police response. For example, the peak age of offending for indictable offences for males in England and Wales in 1998 was 18, and the international evidence shows clearly that many forms of criminal behaviour have their onset in the early teenage years.[166] There is good evidence that theft and burglary rates increase in tandem with the number of young males in society. A recent study found that for every one per cent increase in the number of males aged between 15 and 20, burglary and theft in England and Wales increased by about one per cent.[167]

In addition to efforts to document and explain individual demographic correlates of crime, researchers have devoted extensive attention to the effects of population structure on crime. The most straightforward implication of population structure for crime involves 'compositional effects'. If persons with differing demographic characteristics are at higher or lower risk of criminal involvement, then some of the variation in levels of crime across societies will be due to differences in population composition, i.e. the relative sizes of the respective demographic groups.

According to the Central Statistics Office, the population in April 1999 was 3.74m, the highest level recorded since the census of 1881, when it stood at 3.87m. The final years of the twentieth century saw Ireland transformed into a country of net inward migration, as Figure 21 shows.

If we look at this population change in a little more detail, it can be seen that the number of young males, particularly in the criminogenic 15–24 age cohort, has been increasing over the past decade (see Figure 22). This would lead us to expect an increase in crime, rather than the decrease that has occurred. The demographic factor does not therefore appear to hold in the Irish case as it does elsewhere.

## Drugs and Crime

There are three basic explanatory models for the relationship between drug use and crime: (1) substance use leads to crime, (2) crime leads to substance use and (3) the relationship is either

Figure 21: Net Migration, 1990–1999

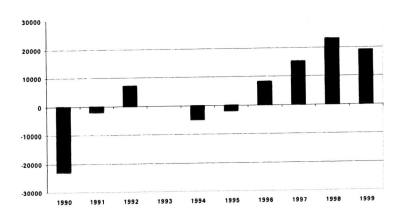

*Source*: Central Statistics Office, *Population and Migration Estimates*, (Dublin: CSO, 1999)

Figure 22: Estimated Male Population
by Age Cohorts, 1990–1999

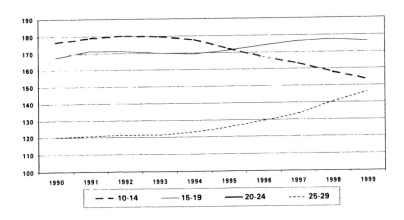

*Source*: Central Statistics Office, *Population and Migration Estimates*, (Dublin, CSO, 1999)

coincidental or explained by a set of common causes.[168] In a detailed review of the literature on the relationship between drugs and crime, White and Gorman argued that:

- Drugusers, and even drug addicts, are heterogeneous in terms of their levels and patterns of criminality.
- Offenders are heterogeneous in terms of their levels and patterns of drug use.
- Most drugusers do not commit any crimes, with the exception of possession and dealing.
- For most criminally involved drug-users, drug use does not cause initial criminal involvement.
- Alcohol is the drug most often associated with violent crime.
- It is not the type of drug per se, but rather the economic conditions of the drug market that appear to influence the drug-crime connection.[169]

The number of drugusers who live in Dublin is uncertain. Various estimates have been made over the years and a recent study suggests that the figure could be higher than 13,000.[170] While little research has been conducted in Ireland specifically on the link between drugs and crime, Keogh has estimated that between September 1995 and August 1996, 66 per cent of all detected crime in the Dublin Metropolitan Area was committed by known 'hard drug' users.[171] Over 80 per cent of burglaries, larcenies from the person and larcenies from unattended vehicles were committed by this group.

Since Keogh carried out his research, the numbers in methadone maintenance treatment have risen. Farrell has argued in relation to methadone treatment in the greater Dublin region, that it is:

> probably one of the more innovative community drug service programmes in Europe. It has taken the core of the evidence on the effectiveness of methadone mainten-ance and attempted to develop a range of services to ensure higher levels of treatment access. This has resulted in a major expansion in the levels of provision

of methadone treatment with over 4,000 individuals in treatment by October 1999.[172]

Given that there is considerable evidence that shows a consistent, statistically significant relationship between maintenance treatment and the reduction of illicit opiate use and drug and property crimes, these programmes are likely to have contributed to the decline in crime, particularly in Dublin.[173] For example, in 1996 there were 1,104 robberies and aggravated burglaries where syringes were used in the commission of the offence. This figure dropped to 442 in 1998 and 298 for the first nine months of 1999.

Furthermore, a recent study of drug-using prostitutes indicated that an increasing number had entered prostitution in order to 'make money for drugs', perhaps as an alternative to acquisitive crime. Shoplifting was becoming more difficult as a result of increased security in city centre retail outlets.[175]

From this brief review it would appear that the factors that may have resulted in the decrease in crime in Ireland are not primarily related to criminal justice policies, but rather to labour market and health policies. Increased employment and consumer expenditure, allied to a growth in methadone treatment would appear to offer more convincing explanations for the decrease. Between 1995 and 1999, recorded crime declined by 29 per cent in the Dublin region and we suggest that improved methadone maintenance programmes, in the wider context of a consumer boom, may have contributed to this drop. It is worth reiterating that the decrease in recorded crime is largely due to a drop in the less serious offences against property (especially larcenies). It conceals a steady rise in crimes against the person.

## 5. The Changing Political Response to Crime

We have seen that the reduction in recorded crime in recent years is open to a variety of interpretations and emphases. However, there is little doubt about the harshness of the current response to crime. Regardless of whether the underlying rate of crime is really going up or down, 'zero tolerance' politics clearly appeals to the current coalition government of Fianna Fáil and the Progressive Democrats. An interesting question is why a punitive consensus has become so firmly embedded in the body politic. Why have law and order issues moved centre stage? Why are dissenting viewpoints so swiftly and effectively ignored?

One explanation is crudely empirical. This holds that harsh policies are required in Ireland because there is a serious problem with crime and this problem is becoming more acute. As crime rates go up, and the public demand a tough response, repressive policies bear down. There is little evidence to support this hypothesis. As we have seen from Garda reports and international figures, Ireland is much safer than other European countries. Furthermore, harsh policies were adopted after crime rates had begun to fall! The tough talk of the 1997 general election campaign took place at a time when the crime rate was already beginning to slide.

The Garda statistics for the previous year are usually published in August. As the 1997 general election took place in June, it is likely that there was no great public awareness at this time that crime was falling. This is borne out by the opinion poll data cited earlier. In its policy document, *Securing a Safer Society*, published in May 1997, Fine Gael made only passing reference to the fact that, 'For the first time since 1989, indictable crime is decreasing.'

Another explanation is psephological. This suggests that opinion surveys show the public want toughness and the politicians have given way to this demand. By recruiting more police and demanding less tolerance they are simply respecting the public will. This is democracy at work. There is little supporting evidence for this view either. In general the public are relatively-ill-informed about the extent of crime and the nature of the response to it. They base their opinions primarily on what they learn from the mass media with the result that they regard heinous crime and bizarre sentences as the norm and believe crime rates are rising when they are falling.[176] In this context, it is not surprising that they demand a firm response.

More sophisticated examination shows that the public tend to have ambivalent attitudes towards crime and punishment. They want offenders punished and rehabilitated, would be prepared to accept tax increases to allow more treatment programmes, but not for prison-building projects, accept the need to imprison some violent offenders but would like to see a wider use of community sanctions and measures.

More importantly it seems clear from the American evidence that it is the preoccupation among politicians with crime issues that causes citizens to become concerned and not *vice versa*. Interestingly, 'those who are less afraid of crime typically express the highest levels of support for the "get tough" approach while those who are more fearful are often less punitive. Rural white men, for example, feel relatively safe but are quite staunch supporters of law and order policies.'[177]

According to Katherine Beckett from the University of Indiana:

> Public support for punitive anti-crime policies is also more fluid and ambivalent than is commonly supposed. Enthusiasm for the death penalty, for example, is historically variable, weakens considerably in the presence of alternatives, and coexists with widespread support for rehabilitative ideals. When given a choice, most Americans still believe that spending money on education and job-training programs is a more effective crime-fighting measure than building prisons. While the punitive tone of the law and order discourse clearly resonates with salient sentiments in American political culture, popular beliefs about crime and punishment are complex, equivocal, and contradictory, even after decades of political initiative on these subjects. The notion that the desire for punishment is ubiquitous and unequivocal ignores the complexity of cultural attitudes and the situational and political factors that shape that expression.[178]

Beckett's thesis contains two main strands. First, that levels of public concern are largely unrelated to the reported incidence of crime but strongly associated with the extent to which the crime issue is highlighted in political discourse. Second, that anxiety about crime does not necessarily give rise to punitiveness.

There are important lessons here for governments formulating crime policies. First, they have a duty to moderate their comments so that they do not create a fear which is disproportionate to risk and difficult to assuage. Second, if the public appears fearful, harshness is not the only response they are likely to accept. There will also be a willingness to consider therapeutic or restorative alternatives. There is plenty of scope for governments to innovate and show compassion. For example, in explaining how Finland, has consistently reduced its prison population (see Table 8 on p. 61), it was argued that, 'The decisive factor in Finland was the attitudinal readiness of the civil servants, the judiciary and the prison authorities to use all available means in order to bring down the number of prisoners.'[179] Other key factors appear to have been the media, which adopted a sober and reasonable attitude towards issues of criminal justice, and collaboration with and assistance from the judiciary.[180]

Television and newspapers are the most important source of information about social issues like crime and punishment. The media's reproduction of the official view of crime probably generates support for policies aimed at punishment rather than prevention. This does not have to be the case and a widening of the debate is clearly in the public interest. The Finnish experience was that: 'The more exposure people have to non-sensationalistic accounts of real criminal incidents (from court documents rather than media accounts), the less punitive they become.'[181]

Politicians, especially in Fianna Fáil, have used crime as a 'wedge issue' designed to separate voters from opposition parties. Criminal justice policy is no longer a subject for practitioners and technocrats. It is no longer an unglamorous core function of government, like public health, transport or education. It has become politicised and emotionally charged.

The wedge was driven home during the penal auction that characterised the 1997 general election. This was a glaring example of political opportunism. Public fears were stoked and simple solutions were offered. A war would be waged on crime and 'zero tolerance' shown to law-breakers. Few attempts were made to provide dispassionate assessments of crime trends and victimisation risks. Sound-bite politics was the order of the day. While slogans and symbols may have some visceral appeal, they do little to solve complex problems. Their attractiveness to politicians lies in their simplicity. To describe the nuances of a rational response to crime requires time and this is impossible to do in a ten-second sound bite. To some extent therefore, the media agenda (especially television and radio) shapes the political discourse in the sense that it makes proper discussion a luxury. To be heard above the crowd requires a mastery of catch-phrases rather than a detailed understanding.

No one is trying to wrest the mantle of 'zero tolerance' from John O'Donoghue. He has shown an impressive ability to persuade the government of the value of his approach and has secured unprecedented levels of financial support (see Table 3, p. 17).

It is to its credit that Fine Gael has not attempted to outdo the government since its return to the opposition benches. Its recent policy documents have focused on crime prevention, restorative justice, the soaring costs of criminal justice and the dubious value of the current prison-building programme.[182] The Labour Party has been reticent in developing alternative criminal justice policies.

This restraint by the opposition parties is an important brake on further excesses and is quite different to the situation in other countries where crime continues to be a significant party political issue. In Britain a Labour Home Secretary is presiding over a steady growth in the prison population. In the USA, both Republicans and Democrats are frightened of being perceived as 'soft' on crime. To be opposed to capital punishment is widely considered to spell disaster at the polls.

Writing about the situation in the United States, sociologists Theodore Caplow and Jonathan Simon argue that American politics has moved away from traditional divisions, based on class and region, towards a range of single-issue movements based on abortion, capital punishment, gay rights, gun control and so on.[183] These controversies do not easily give up to compromise. The debate is always polarised and the electorate is fragmented. This is binary politics – you are with us or against us. It is difficult for politicians to take a stance without alienating people at one extreme. This has encouraged elected representatives to campaign on issues that command broad support – such as cracking down on crime, putting more people behind bars and limiting immigration. No one is in favour of more crime, so harsh policies are likely to offend few significant constituencies and generate broad-based and visceral support. It is also a simple fact of political life that it is easier to generate support against something than for something.

If harsh laws are enacted after crime rates have begun to fall, this may trick people into believing that the harsh measures have worked. This may well be the case in Ireland in ten years' time, when the correlation between a growing prison population and a falling crime rate is seen as cause and effect rather than effect and cause. It is also possible, of course, that people do not care whether harsh crime policies 'work'. They support them for 'expressive' reasons. They are interested in denunciation, in highlighting wrongdoing regardless of the consequences.

## Are we Witnessing the Growth of a 'Crime Complex'?

David Garland, a leading theorist of punishment, has reflected on the meaning behind recent developments in criminal justice policy around the world. His insights may be of value in considering contemporary Ireland. He argues that,

> Despite the fact that crime has an uneven social distribution, and that high risk victimisation is very much a pocketed, concentrated phenomenon, crime is widely

> experienced as a prominent fact of modern life. For most people, crime is no longer an aberration or an unexpected, abnormal event. Instead, the threat of crime has become a routine part of modern consciousness, an everyday risk. . . . My claim is that the normality of high crime rates in late modern society has prompted a series of transformations in official perceptions of crime, in criminological discourse, in modes of governmental action, and in the structure of criminal justice organisations.[184]

Developing on this theme, Garland has identified a 'crime complex' which he believes characterises modern societies.[185] This complex is based on a number of distinctive characteristics:

- high crime rates are a normal social fact;
- emotional investment in crime issues is widespread and intense: people are angry, anxious and fascinated;
- crime issues are politicised and publicly represented in emotive terms;
- common sense replaces expert opinion;
- concerns about victims and public safety dominate policy discussions;
- the criminal justice system is seen as inadequate or ineffective;
- private, defensive routines are widespread and there is a large market in private security;
- crime consciousness is all pervasive.

Once established, this worldview is difficult to change, even in the face of declining crime rates. It creates a social context that is receptive to punitive 'solutions'. It is fertile ground for the politics of 'zero tolerance'.

In Britain and the United States of America this context appears to be firmly established. As a result a public tolerance, and even appetite, has been whetted for approaches to crime which twenty years ago would have been considered outrageous – for example, the revival of chain gangs and corporal punishment, boot camps, the imprisonment of children, electronic tagging, mandatory minimum sentences and austere prisons.

A complex interplay of political cynicism, public frustration, rapid social change and growing feelings of insecurity may propel Ireland towards the development of Garland's 'crime complex'. The McCabe and Guerin murders, the response to them and the context they helped to generate may have launched us on this trajectory.

Although these killings had serious repercussions, it was not inevitable that they would lead to the politics of 'zero tolerance'. It is possible to imagine a range of other responses – refocusing of Garda activity rather than recruitment of more gardaí; proper treatment for heroin addicts to reduce the demand for drugs and thus the incentive to trade in them; provision of opportunities to disadvantaged young men to reduce the likelihood that they will opt for a life of crime. This could all have occurred in parallel with finding the killers and bringing them to justice. However, the response was swift, harsh, uncompromising and skewed towards punishment.[186]

This reaction was very similar to the response to the mugging described in the book *Policing the Crisis*. On 5 November 1972, Robert Keenan was walking home from a pub in Birmingham. He met three boys who stopped him and asked for a cigarette. They knocked him to the ground and dragged him to a nearby piece of waste land, where they robbed him of 30 pence, some keys and five cigarettes. Two hours later they returned and attacked him, this time with a brick. Again they left, only to return once more to complete the onslaught. The ringleader, Paul Storey (aged 16), pleaded guilty to robbery and attempted murder and was sentenced to 20 years. This exemplary sentence was passed at a time of growing hysteria about 'mugging'.

*Policing the Crisis* examined the political, economic and ideological dimensions of mugging in particular and crime in general. It showed how the media and judicial reaction to Paul Storey helped to legitimate a more coercive state role in a period of growing conflict based on class and race.[187] The McCabe and Guerin killings may have served a similar purpose in this country, although for different reasons.

## Suppressing Dissent

Another interesting facet of contemporary approaches to crime and punishment is the extent to which dissenting voices are silenced or ignored. Since the current government took office in 1997, several major reports have taken issue with the thrust of its policies and offered an alternative vision. However, these reports appear to have had little impact on policy. Even more worryingly, a number of expert groups and forums have reported to the Minister for Justice, Equality and Law Reform since he assumed office and their advice has been largely ignored. For example, the Expert Group on the Probation and Welfare Service criticised the prison-building programme advocated by the minister and called for a range of social measures to curb crime.[188] The Report of the Oireachtas Sub-Committee on *Alternatives to Fines and the Uses of Prison* argued that 'Greater recourse to imprisonment is not the only way in which the problem of crime can be addressed.'[189]

The National Crime Forum was established by the Minister for Justice, Equality and Law Reform in February 1998. In his opening remarks, John O'Donoghue said he saw the work of the Forum as part of his 'total war on crime'. Its brief was to solicit views on crime and related matters from the general public as well as national and international experts.[190] This broad cross section of opinion would then be reflected back to the Minister and used to inform the development of crime policy. This mechanism would make government aware of the public's mood on law and order matters.

Under the chairmanship of Professor Bryan McMahon, the Forum held public meetings in Dublin, Cork, Limerick and Sligo. It considered 250 written submissions and 88 oral presentations. The Forum's report was completed with commendable speed and published in December 1998. While it does not contain any specific recommendations, a number of interesting themes emerge. The fact that the views put forward in the report have been distilled from a wide cross section of opinion gives them great moral authority.

Perhaps the most important theme was that while there may be a crime problem, it is not one of crisis proportions and the public is not calling for draconian action. There was very little popular support for the hardline political rhetoric that has been so typical of the debate about crime in recent years.[191]

The report contained a plea for debate about the proper place of the prison in society. 'The Forum endorses the call for a fundamental change of focus to make prison the option of last resort, to be used sparingly and only when all other options have been tried or considered and ruled out for cogent reasons.'[192] The need for research and information was repeated frequently.

Those who addressed the Forum displayed a sensitivity to the complexities of the crime problem, which was in striking contrast to the simplistic reductionism that too often passes for political debate. While there is no doubt that their call was for effective action, this was not equated with more Garda powers or longer prison sentences. Their desire was for understanding rather than condemnation. There is a vital lesson here for those charged with policy formulation. It is that political strategies that respond to a perceived thirst for vengeance may be based on a misreading of the public mood.

## What Does it All Mean?

Predicting social trends is a highly imprecise science. The task is even more fraught with uncertainty when the available data are scarce, of poor quality and highly politicised. Nevertheless, we may be able to draw a few tentative conclusions from existing criminological research. Acknowledging the limited application of Field's model, if it applies to Ireland, the current economic boom should lead – in the short term – to dropping rates of property crime (and thus a reduction in the overall level of recorded crime), while the number of crimes of violence against the person will grow. We should be alert to the fact that a falling crime rate during a time of increasing consumption may conceal within it increases in the patterns of recorded (e.g. violence against the person), and unrecorded (e.g. white collar and corporate) crime.

If accurate, this is a worrying forecast, especially given that we already resort to imprisonment more frequently than our European neighbours. There is a risk of descending into the 'populist punitiveness' which characterises the response to crime in Britain and the United States. The trend in these countries is for tough political rhetoric to lead to a hardening in public and judicial attitudes, a rise in public anxiety and an explosion in the size of the prison population. The dangers of such policies for the poor and the marginalised are captured in the growth of the penal-industrial complex described by Nils Christie, who argues that 'The major dangers of crime in modern societies are not the crimes, but that the fight against them may lead societies toward totalitarian developments.'[193]

Perhaps we must accept that we will never fully understand complex social problems. As one leading penologist has put it: 'It is not "crime" or even criminological knowledge about crime which most affects policy decisions, but rather the ways in which "the crime problem" is officially perceived and the political positions to which these perceptions give rise.'[194] Crime-related issues are socially and politically constructed and acquire their meaning though interpretation, symbols and debate. They have no independent life.

However, it would be going too far to suggest that everything is open to conflicting interpretation. There are a small number of areas where there is no great dispute, and these are at the centre of the arguments put forward in this book and summarised in our introduction.

The purpose of this book has been to stimulate critical thought about recent criminal justice policies in Ireland. In the absence of informed debate it is possible that in years to come politicians will claim that 'zero tolerance', as expressed through heavy policing of low level disorder and an expansion of prison capacity, caused a reduction in crime. This could be used as the excuse for even more repressive measures when the cycle of crime turns upward again, as it inevitably will. This ratcheting up of the stakes will bring us another step closer to a society where our lives are shaped in myriad ways by reactions to crime.

It would be simplistic to attempt to identify a single cause of recent policy shifts. However, the role of John O'Donoghue in opposition and in government, over the past five years, has been critical. His policies have reshaped the criminal justice and penal systems. He must take a large measure of the responsibility for the surge in the prison population and the promotion of intolerance as public policy.

It would be unrealistic to expect any government to be able to remove the motivations to offend, whether this involves a street mugging or non-payment of tax. What can be controlled, however, are the responses to crime, which may contain within them some solutions. The key issue is that something can be done, that the management of punishment is within political control. The amount we punish and how we punish does not emerge as if by magic from underlying crime trends.

Politicians do not have the power to affect crime rates directly, at least in the short term, but they do have the power to influence the nature of the response to crime and the tone of the debate about its consequences. The responsible use of this power is in the interests of humanity, justice and economy.

# Notes and References

1  IMS survey carried out between 01/06/80 and 10/06/80 for *The Irish Times*.

2  IMS survey carried out between 08/04/88 and 10/04/88 for Independent Newspapers.

3  Lansdowne survey carried out on 24/11/94 for *The Sunday Press*.

4  IMS survey carried out on 04/07/96 for *The Sunday Independent*.

5  IMS survey carried out on 17/12/96 for *The Irish Independent*.

6  MRBI survey carried out between 27/01/97 and 28/01/97 for *The Irish Times*.

7  For a critique of the limitations of opinion polls, see P. Bourdieu, 'Public Opinion Does Not Exist', in P. Bourdieu (ed.), *Sociology in Question* (London: Sage, 1993).

8  S. Cohen, *Folk Devils and Moral Panics: The Creation of the Mods and Rockers* (Oxford: Martin Robinson, 1980), p. 9. Three unrelated rural killings in January 1996 had set the scene for this 'moral panic'. See C. McCullagh, 'Rural Crime in the Republic of Ireland', in G. Dingwall and S.R. Moody (eds.), *Crime and Conflict in the Countryside* (Cardiff: University of Wales Press, 1999).

9  *Leading the Fight Against Crime: A Fianna Fáil Position Paper on Justice*, (Dublin: Fianna Fáil, 1997), p. 2.

10  Dáil Debates, 15 November 1983.

11  R. Byrne et al., *Innocent Till Proven Guilty?* (Dublin: Irish Council for Civil Liberties, 1983).

12  T. O'Malley, *Sentencing Law and Practice* (Dublin: Round Hall Sweet and Maxwell, 2000), p. xiii.

13  Examples include the MAY project, the ABLE project, the WEB project, the NICKOL project, the MATES project and the BALL project. These are part of a network of Garda special projects which claim to divert young people away from crime through the operation of a combination of intervention and prevention programmes.

14  Court mediation projects were established by the Department of Justice, Equality and Law Reform in Tallaght (Co. Dublin) and Nenagh (Co. Tipperary) in 1999.

15  Government of Ireland, *Sharing in Progress: National Anti-Poverty Strategy* (Dublin: Stationery Office, 1997).

16  Drug Court Planning Committee, *First Report of the Pilot Project* (Dublin: Stationery Office, 1999).

17   P. O'Malley, 'Volatile and Contradictory Punishment', *Theoretical Criminology*, vol. 3, no. 2, 1999, pp. 175–196.

18   G. Burchell, 'Liberal Government and Techniques of the Self', in A. Barry et al. (eds.), *Foucault and Political Reason: Liberalism, Neo-Liberalism and Rationalities of Government* (University College London Press, 1996).

19   Health and Safety Authority, *Annual Report 1999* (Dublin: HSA, 2000), p. 13.

20   *The Irish Times*, 18 November 1997.

21   Department of Social, Community and Family Affairs, *Annual Report 1998* (Dublin: Stationery Office, 1999).

22   Revenue Commissioners, *Statistical Report for the Year Ended 31st December 1998* (Dublin: Stationery Office, 1999), p. 107.

23   The Housing (Miscellaneous Provisions) Act 1997 defines antisocial behaviour as: '(a) the manufacture, production, preparation, importation, exportation, sale or supply, or distribution of a controlled drug; and (b) any behaviour which causes or is likely to cause any significant or persistent danger, injury, damages, loss or fear to any person living, working or otherwise lawfully in the vicinity of a house provided by a housing authority under the Housing Acts 1966 to 1997, or a housing estate in which the house is situated and, without prejudice to the foregoing, includes violence, threats, intimidation, coercion, harassment or serious obstruction of any person'.

24   Consultative Group on the Private Security Industry, *Report* (Dublin: Stationery Office, 1997), p. 19.

25   L. McNiffe, *A History of the Garda Síochána* (Dublin: Wolfhound Press, 1997). It should also be noted that they were, and remain, primarily male servants of the people with females not allowed to enter the ranks until 1959. Only in the last decade has there been a noticeable increase in the numbers of female gardaí. For further information, see J. Brown, 'Discriminatory Experiences of Women Police: A Comparison of Officers Serving in England and Wales, Scotland, Northern Ireland and the Republic of Ireland', *International Journal of the Sociology of Law*, vol. 28, no. 2, 2000, pp. 91–11.

26   The reference periods used throughout this book are wherever possible 1960 to 1999 (to indicate long-term trends) and 1990 to 1999 (to highlight more recent developments).

27   A range of well-known difficulties faces researchers attempting to analyse crime data across countries. Varying definitions of crime,

inconsistent recording and operating practices are only some of the more stubborn problems. Comparative analyses must be treated with caution. Despite these caveats, such comparisons do assist us to question received practices in Ireland and highlight local concerns. More importantly, they help us to understand what priorities different countries place on different offences. See, for example, J. van Dijk and K. Kangaspunta, 'Piecing Together the Cross-National Crime Puzzle', *National Institute of Justice Journal*, 2000, pp. 35–41.

28  Prior to this date crime figures can be found in the annual *Statistical Abstracts of Ireland*.

29  For a pioneering article, see D.J. Black, 'Production of Crime Rates', *American Sociological Review*, vol. 35, no. 4, 1970, pp. 733–48.

30  J. Muncie, 'The Construction and Deconstruction of Crime', in J. Muncie and E. McLaughlin (eds.), *The Problem of Crime* (London: Sage, 1996).

31  H. Schwendinger and J. Schwendinger, 'Defenders of Order or Guardians of Human Rights?', in I. Taylor, P. Walton and J. Young (eds.), *Critical Criminology* (London: Routledge and Kegan Paul, 1975).

32  Department of Justice, *Tackling Crime – Discussion Paper* (Dublin: Stationery Office, 1997), p. 10.

33  These distinctions were drawn up by British parliamentary statutes in 1849 and 1851.

34  The new Garda computer system (PULSE) was supposed to cost £23.6m. The budget was revised upwards to £36m and again to £55.6m, but still overran, despite being scaled down in size and located in 161 stations instead of 242. See Comptroller and Auditor General, *Annual Report*, vol. 1 (Dublin: Stationery Office, 2000), p. 57.

35  D.B. Rottman, *Crime in the Republic of Ireland: Statistical Trends and their Interpretation*, Paper No. 102 (Dublin: Economic and Social Research Institute, 1980), p. 37.

36  For an analysis of crime in Ireland prior to 1960, see P. Hillyard, *The Nature and Extent of Crime in Ireland*, Unpublished Masters Thesis (University of Keele, 1969).

37  M. O'Connell, 'The Volume of Crime in Ireland – Crime Surveys and Official Figures', *Irish Criminal Law Journal*, vol. 10, no. 2, 2000, pp. 7–11.

38  Steering Group on the Efficiency and Effectiveness of the Garda Síochána, *Report* (Dublin: Stationery Office, 1997), p. 32.

39   See L. Radzinowicz and J. King, *The Growth of Crime: The International Experience* (Harmondsworth: Pelican, 1979).

40   J. Young, *The Exclusive Society: Social Exclusion, Crime and Difference in Late Modernity* (London: Sage, 1999), p. 122.

41   As Elliot Currie has pointed out, while most accounts of rising crime rates in post-communist countries rightly highlight the link between crime and the disintegration of social safety nets, they seem unable to make the same link in market oriented societies. As he shrewdly puts it: 'There is a kind of schizoid willingness to see the negative social impact of the heedless drive to an unfettered market when it is going on in someone else's country – but not in ours. We are able to recognise the disruptive impact of the unleashing of the market in Shanghai but not in St Louis; in Leningrad, but not in Los Angeles'. E. Currie, 'Market, Crime and Community: Towards a Mid-range Theory of Post-Industrial Violence', *Theoretical Criminology*, vol. 1, no. 2, 1997, p. 148.

42   For an early analysis of the economics of crime control in Ireland, see P. Bacon and M. O'Donoghue, 'The Economics of Crime in Ireland: An Exploratory Paper', *Economic and Social Review*, vol. 7, no. 1, 1975, pp. 19–34.

43   Expenditure on the gardaí represents approximately two-thirds of the total criminal justice expenditure in any given year.

44   For further information, see T. O'Malley, *Sexual Offences: Law Policy and Punishment* (Dublin: Round Hall Sweet and Maxwell, 1996); C. Leon, 'Recorded Sexual Offences in Ireland 1994–1997: An Overview', *Irish Criminal Law Journal*, vol. 10, no. 3, 2000, pp. 2–7.

45   For a more detailed analysis of homicide trends in Ireland, see E. Dooley, *Homicide in Ireland 1972–1991* (Dublin: Stationery Office, 1995).

46   E. Currie, 'Market, Crime and Community: Towards a Mid-range Theory of Post-Industrial Violence', *Theoretical Criminology*, vol. 1, no. 2, 1997, pp. 147–72.

47   H. Croall, *White Collar Crime* (Buckingham: Open University Press, 1992), p. 3.

48   For an early discussion on white collar crime in Ireland, see D.B. Rottman and P.F. Tormey, 'Respectable Crime: Occupational and Professional Crime in the Republic of Ireland', *Studies*, vol. 75, no. 297, 1986, pp. 43–55.

49   C. McCullagh, *Crime in Ireland: A Sociological Introduction* (Cork University Press, 1996), p. 66.

50 See, for example, A. Sherriff et al., 'The Dunnes Payments Scandal, Charles Haughey and Contemporary Irish Political Culture', *Crime, Law and Social Change*, vol. 30, 1998, pp. 43–65; Public Accounts Committee, *Parliamentary Inquiry into D.I.R.T.*, First Report (Dublin: Stationery Office, 1999).

51 For a detailed analysis of the manner in which Garda figures are produced, see D. Watson, *Victims of Recorded Crime in Ireland: Results from the 1996 Survey* (Dublin: ESRI/Oaktree Press, 2000), pp. 16–20.

52 L. Radzinowicz, 'English Criminal Statistics', in L. Radzinowicz and J.W.C. Turner (eds.), *The Modern Approach to Criminal Law* (London: Macmillan, 1945), p. 193.

53 M. Maguire, 'Crime Statistics, Patterns, and Trends: Changing Interpretations and their Implications', in M. Maguire, R. Morgan and R. Reiner (eds.), *The Oxford Handbook of Criminology*, 2nd edn (Oxford University Press, 1997), p. 164.

54 See, for example, R. Breen and D.B. Rottman, *Crime Victimisation in the Republic of Ireland* (Dublin: Economic and Social Research Institute, 1985); M. O'Connell and A. Whelan, 'Crime Victimisation in Dublin', *Irish Criminal Law Journal*, vol. 4, no. 1, 1994, pp. 85–112.

55 M. O'Connell, 'The Volume of Crime in Ireland: Crime Surveys and Official Figures', *Irish Criminal Law Journal*, vol. 10, no. 2, 2000, pp. 7–11.

56 Central Statistics Office, *Quarterly National Household Survey – Crime and Victimisation* (Dublin: CSO, 1999).

57 These figures must be interpreted with caution. The number of crimes reported to gardaí is based on the reporting rate in the CSO report. The Garda figure for burglary includes aggravated burglary and armed aggravated burglary. The Garda figure for theft of motor vehicle, includes larceny of cars, motor cycles, lorries and other vehicles (all indictable offences), and taking a vehicle without authority and unauthorised interference with mechanism of motor vehicle (both non-indictable). The reference period in the CSO survey was the twelve months to November 1998, while the Garda statistics relate to the calendar year 1998.

58 D. Watson, *Victims of Recorded Crime in Ireland: Results from the 1996 Survey* (Dublin: Economic and Social Research Institute/Oaktree Press, 2000) found that some victims denied having reported a crime, and a significant number claimed to have reported a crime which differed from that recorded by the Garda.

59   See, for example, C. Clarkson et al., 'Assaults: The Relationship between Seriousness, Criminalisation and Punishment', *Criminal Law Review,* vol. 57, 1994, pp. 4–20.

60   There are considerable methodological difficulties in measuring 'fear of crime' and the phrase has been equated with a variety of emotional states, attitudes, or perceptions (including mistrust of others, anxiety, perceived risk, fear of strangers, or concern about deteriorating neighborhoods or declining national morality). See S. Walklate, 'Excavating the Fear of Crime: Fear, Anxiety or Trust?', *Theoretical Criminology,* vol. 2, no. 4, 1998, pp. 403–18.

61   D. McDade, *Public Perception of Crime in Ireland* (Research and Evaluation Services, 1999).

62   M. Hough and P. Mayhew, *The 1982 British Crime Survey* (London: HMSO, 1983).

63   M. Warr, 'Fear of Crime in the United States: Avenues for Research and Policy', *Criminal Justice 2000 Vol. 4: Measurement and Analysis of Crime and Justice* (US Department of Justice, 2000).

64   M. O'Connell and A. Whelan, 'Crime Victimisation in Dublin', *Irish Criminal Law Journal,* vol. 4, no. 1, 1994, pp. 85–112; M. O'Connell and A. Whelan, 'Taking Wrongs Seriously: Public Perceptions of Crime Seriousness', *British Journal of Criminology,* vol. 36, no. 2, 1996, pp. 299–318; M. O'Connell et al., 'Newspaper Readership and the Perception of Crime: Testing an Assumed Relationship through a Triangulation of Methods', *Legal and Criminological Psychology,* vol. 3, 1998, pp. 29–57.

65   G. Kerrigan and H. Shaw, 'Crime Hysteria', *Magill,* 18 April 1985.

66   Department of Justice, *The Management of Offenders: A Five-Year Plan* (Dublin: Stationery Office, 1994).

67   Whitaker Committee, *Report of the Committee of Inquiry into the Penal System* (Dublin: Stationery Office, 1985).

68   Department of Justice, *Tackling Crime: A Discussion Paper* (Dublin: Stationery Office, 1997), p. 5.

69   Speech in April 1997, referred to in opening address to National Crime Forum.

70   See, for example, P. O'Mahony, *Criminal Chaos: Seven Crises in Irish Criminal Justice* (Dublin: Round Hall Sweet and Maxwell, 1996).

71   S. King and R. Wilford, 'Irish Political Data 1996', *Irish Political Studies,* vol. 12, 1997, pp. 123–147.

72   M. Cavadino and J. Dignan, *The Penal System: An Introduction,* 2nd edn (London: Sage, 1997), pp. 100–3.

73  R. Reiner, 'Crime and Control in Britain', *Sociology*, vol. 34, 2000, pp. 71–94.

74  *The Irish Times*, 12 March 1997.

75  J.Q. Wilson and G. Kelling, 'Broken Windows', *Atlantic Monthly*, March 1982, pp. 29–38; G. Kelling and C. Coles, *Fixing Broken Windows: Restoring Order and Reducing Crime in Our Communities* (New York: Free Press, 1996).

76  This view has been challenged. Recent research has highlighted the limited returns from aggressive police strategies in terms of a reduction in robbery and aggravated burglary. See, for example, K.J. Novak et al., 'The Effects of Aggressive Policing of Disorder on Serious Crime', *Policing: An International Journal of Police Strategies and Management*, vol. 22, no. 2, 1999, pp. 171–90.

77  For further details, see N. Bland and T. Read, *Policing Anti-Social Behaviour* (London: Home Office Policing and Reducing Crime Unit, 2000).

78  A. Crawford, *The Local Governance of Crime: Appeals to Community and Partnerships* (Oxford: Clarendon Press, 1997).

79  M. Erikson, *Report on the Need to Establish a European Union Wide Campaign for Zero Tolerance of Violence against Women* (Brussels: Committee on Women's Rights, 1997).

80  G. Pearson, 'Lawlessness, Modernity and Social Change: A Historical Appraisal', *Theory, Culture and Society*, vol. 2, no. 3, 1985, pp. 15–16.

81  For Bratton's self-serving account of how his policies reduced crime, see W. Bratton and P. Knobler, *Turnaround: How America's Top Cop Reversed the Crime Epidemic* (New York: Random House, 1998).

82  Bratton went on to become president and chief operating officer of the CARCO Group Inc., a New York-based information services firm.

83  *Sunday Times*, News Review, 22 March 1998.

84  W. Bratton, 'Crime is Down in New York City: Blame the Police', in N. Dennis (ed.), *Zero Tolerance: Policing a Free Society*, 2nd edn (London: Institute for Economic Affairs, 1998).

85  M. Innes, 'An Iron Fist in an Iron Glove? The Zero Tolerance Policing Debate', *The Howard Journal*, vol. 38, no. 4, 1999, pp. 397–410.

86  Given the fact that computerisation in Garda stations was virtually non-existent when 'zero tolerance' was being touted, it could never have worked. Pencil and paper records are not an adequate basis for the high-technology requirements of 'zero tolerance' policing.

Similarly, it is difficult to imagine the Garda culture being conducive to high levels of mobility among senior officers on the basis of objective measures of their performance.

87   *Sunday Times*, News Review, 22 March 1998.

88   Between 1993 and 1996 there was a decline in crime in 17 of 25 of the largest US cities. In some there had been no change in policing, in others less aggressive policies were adopted and in others 'zero tolerance' was the driving force. See, for example, J. Young, *The Exclusive Society: Social Exclusion, Crime and Difference in Late Modernity* (London: Sage, 1999), p.125; B. Bowling, 'The Rise and Fall of New York Murder: Zero Tolerance or Crack's Decline?', *British Journal of Criminology*, vol. 39, no. 4, 1999, pp. 531–54.

89   P. Grabosky, *Zero Tolerance Policing*, Trends and Issues No. 102 (Canberra: Australian Institute of Criminology, 1999). A controversial new study has linked the reduction in crime in the USA to the legalisation of abortion in 1973. Donohue and Levitt argue that the timing of the reduction 'is consistent with legalized abortion reducing crime rates with a twenty-year lag,' and that the first states to legalise abortion were also the first to experience dropping crime rates. They also note that states with high abortion rates have experienced larger drops in crime than other states since 1985, even after controlling for other factors related to crime. They further argue that, 'The declines in crime in high abortion states are disproportionately concentrated among those under the age of 25', and that if their estimates are correct, 'legalized abortion can explain about half of the recent fall in crime.' (J. Donohoe and S. Levitt, *The Impact of Legalized Abortion on Crime*, Working Paper 8004 (Cambridge, MA: National Bureau of Economic Research, 2000).

90   Bratton did not last three years with the NYPD and was succeeded as Commissioner by Howard Safir in March 1996. His relationship with Mayor Giuliani had been tempestuous from the start, both men hungry to claim the credit for the remarkable fall in New York's crime rate.

91   C. Parenti, *Lockdown America: Police and Prisons in the Age of Crisis* (New York: Verso, 1999), p. 69.

92   Another implication is that complaints against police will rise. Given the already serious concerns about Garda complaints procedures, an increase in the workload of this body is unlikely to promote public respect for the police. See D. Walsh, 'Who Guards the Guards?' *Studies*, vol. 88, no. 350, 1998, pp. 154–163.

93  R. Gooding-Williams (ed.), *Reading Rodney King/Reading Urban Uprising* (London: Routledge, 1993).

94  W.J. Bratton, 'Crime is Down in New York City: Blame the Police', in N. Dennis (ed.), *Zero Tolerance: Policing a Free Society*, 2nd edn (London: Institute for Economic Affairs, 1998), pp. 42–3.

95  *The Irish Times*, 10 March 1997.

96  Steering Group on the Efficiency and Effectiveness of the Garda Síochána, *Report* (Dublin: Stationery Office, 1997).

97  As he made clear to the US House of Representatives *Committee on Government Reform and Oversight* in March 1999, Timoney was an ardent disciple of the approach to fighting crime introduced by Commissioner Bratton. In his testimony, Timoney stated: 'It was as Chief of Department under Commissioner Bratton that I had the good fortune of being a member of the team that changed fundamentally the way in which the NYPD approached its core mission of policing New York. As part of our new approach, we developed an entirely new and much more effective set of policies and procedures for tackling urban crime and disorder.'

98  R. Hopkins Burke, 'The Socio-Political Context of Zero Tolerance Policing Strategies', *Policing: An International Journal of Police Strategies and Management*, vol. 21, no. 4, 1998, pp. 666–82.

99  G. Murphy, 'The 1997 General Election in the Republic of Ireland', *Irish Political Studies*, vol. 13, 1998, pp. 127–34.

100  Dáil debates, 26 June 1997.

101  Press statement, Department of Justice, Equality and Law Reform, 8 August 2000.

102  Department of Justice, Equality and Law Reform, *Strategy Statement 1998–2000: Community Security and Equality* (Dublin: Department of Justice, Equality and Law Reform, 1998).

103  An Garda Síochána, *Evaluation of Policing Plan 1998–99* (Dublin: Stationery Office, 2000), p. 35.

104  Address by John O'Donoghue TD at the launch of the National Crime Forum, 26 February 1998.

105  102,484 indictable crimes were recorded in 1995, the highest number ever.

106  An early chronicler of the Irish prison system, Peadar Cowen, highlighted the high number of prisoners in Ireland who were products of the industrial and reformatory school system. P. Cowen, *Dungeons Deep: A Monograph on Prisons, Borstals, Reformatories and Industrial*

*Schools in the Republic of Ireland, and Some Reflections on Crime and Punishment and Matters Relating Thereto* (Dublin: Marion Printing, 1960).

107   S. Flynn and P. Yeates, *Smack: The Criminal Drugs Racket in Ireland* (Dublin: Gill and Macmillan, 1985), p. 276.

108   R. McCelland, M. Webb and G. Mock, 'Mental Health Services in Ireland', *International Journal of Law and Psychiatry*, vol. 23, no. 3–4, 2000, pp. 309–28.

109   *The Irish Times*, 5 August 2000.

110   The extent of the growth of female involvement in the labour force since the 1970s may be exaggerated as it has been suggested that earlier data seriously underestimated their levels of participation. T. Fahey, 'Measuring the Female Labour Supply: Conceptual and Procedural Problems in Irish Official Statistics', *The Economic and Social Review*, vol. 21, 1990, pp. 163–91.

111   Centre for Research and Development, *Vocations in Ireland*, (Maynooth: CRD, 2000).

112   T. Fahey (ed.), *Social Housing in Ireland: A Study of Success, Failure and Lessons Learned* (Dublin: Oaktree Press, 1999).

113   K.C. Kearns, *Dublin Tenement Life: An Oral History* (Dublin: Gill and Macmillan, 1994).

114   F. Adler, *Nations Not Obsessed with Crime* (Littleton, Co: Rothman, 1983).

115   ibid. p. 11.

116   ibid. p. 133.

117   Strong religious and family controls may conceal crime rather than control it. Adler does not address this issue. See, for example, M. Raftery and E. O'Sullivan, *Suffer the Little Children: The Inside Story of Ireland's Industrial Schools* (Dublin: New Island Books, 1999); S. McKay, *Sophia's Story* (Dublin: Gill and Macmillan, 1998).

118   C. McCullagh, *Crime in Ireland: A Sociological Introduction* (Cork University Press, 1996), pp. 155–56; B. Whelan and M. Murphy, 'Public Attitudes to the Gardaí', *Communique: An Garda Síochána Management Journal*, no. 1, 1994, pp. 15–18.

119   D. Watson, *Victims of Recorded Crime in Ireland: Results from the 1996 Survey* (Dublin: Economic and Social Research Institute/Oaktree Press, 2000), pp. 168–70.

120   ibid. p. 173.

121   For example, D.B. Rottman, *The Criminal Justice System: Policy and Performance*, Report No. 77 (Dublin: National Economic and Social

Council, 1984); P. O'Mahony, *Crime and Punishment in Ireland* (Dublin: Round Hall Press, 1993); J.D. Brewer, B. Lockhart and P. Rodgers, *Crime in Ireland, 1945–95: Here be Dragons* (Oxford: Clarendon Press, 1997). Durkheim's notion of anomie is the basis for many contemporary theories that pinpoint the effects of modernisation as the main cause of crime. Crime is seen as a consequence of defective social regulation. People offend because society offers little in the way of restraint or moral direction. Durkheim argued that, as nations develop, they are characterised by an increasingly intricate web of social and economic relations. These complex divisions are suspected of undermining the 'mechanical solidarity' that characerised simple pre-industrial societies. Thus, rapid social change engenders the breakdown of traditional values, resulting in, among other things, a higher crime rate. Eventually, however, the transition to a more complex form of social organisation ('organic solidarity') and more formal mechanisms of social control should halt rising crime rates, although they are expected to remain at higher levels than before development. The stimulus for modernisation is technological advancement, and this catalyst leads to political, economic, and demographic changes within a society. Industrialisation and urbanisation are key elements of this social transformation. Their effects – which include the tension between groups that accompanies increased social differentiation and the socio-economic inequality many presume to follow modernisation – are viewed as the main contributors to rising crime rates. In general, the overall rate of crime is expected to increase but eventually level off as modernisation progresses, while another expected result is the predominance of property and economic crimes over crimes against the person.

122 C. McCullagh, *Crime in Ireland: A Sociological Introduction* (Cork University Press, 1996), pp. 133–44.

123 For further elaboration on these themes, see H. Tovey and P. Share, *A Sociology of Ireland* (Dublin: Gill and Macmillan, 2000), pp. 256–78.

124 By dependent development, McCullagh means that 'periphery countries do not change by responding to their own needs but by adapting to the requirements of the developed centre. Thus the links which have been established between periphery countries and the developed core create dependent societies in which the possibilities

for autonomous growth are restricted.' C. McCullagh, *Crime in Ireland: A Sociological Introduction* (Cork University Press, 1996), pp. 123–124.

125   Inter-Departmental Group, *Urban Crime and Disorder* (Dublin: Stationery Office, 1992).

126   M. McConville, A. Sanders and R. Leng, *The Case for the Prosecution: Police Suspects and the Construction of Criminality* (London: Routledge, 1991). In relation to how Irish people in Britain were constructed as a criminal community, see P. Hillyard, *Suspect Community: People's Experience of the Prevention of Terrorism Acts in Britain* (London: Pluto, 1993).

127   Hillyard and Gordon have suggested that we pay particular attention to arrest rates as they reveal changes in the character of the criminal justice system. In their analysis in England and Wales, they argue that increasing arrest rates coupled with a substantial decline in the prosecution rate has resulted in a 'radical shift in power away from a formal, open and public system of justice towards an informal and closed system'. P. Hillyard and D. Gordon, 'Arresting Statistics: The Drift to Informal Justice in England and Wales', *Journal of Law and Society*, vol. 26, no. 4, 1999, pp. 502–22.

128   D. B. Rottman, *The Criminal Justice System: Policy and Performance* (Dublin: National Economic and Social Council, 1984).

129   For examples see R. Reiner, *The Politics of the Police*, 2nd edn (Hemel Hempstead: Wheatsheaf, 1992); S. Uglow, *Policing Liberal Society* (Oxford University Press, 1988); R. Morgan and T. Newburn, *The Future of Policing* (Oxford University Press, 1997).

130   R. Reiner, 'Policing and the Police', in M. Maguire, R. Morgan and R. Reiner (eds.), *The Oxford Handbook of Criminology*, 2nd edn (Oxford University Press, 1997), p. 1024.

131   Vagrancy (Ireland) Act 1847, s. 3.

132   G. Kelling and C. Coles, *Fixing Broken Windows: Restoring Order and Reducing Crime in Our Communities* (New York: Free Press, 1996), p. 20.

133   Law Reform Commission, *Report on Vagrancy and Related Offences* (Dublin: Law Reform Commission, 1985), p. 61.

134   J. Swift, *A Critical Essay upon the Faculties of the Mind* (1707).

135   G. Carey, 'The Rule of Law, Public Order Targeting and the Construction of Crime', *Irish Criminal Law Journal*, vol. 8, no. 1, 1998, p. 49.

136 Department of Environment and Local Government, *Annual Housing Statistics Bulletin* (Dublin: Stationery Office, 2000).

137 For an early analysis of the interaction between the homeless and the criminal justice system, see J. O'Brien, *Criminal Neglect – Some Aspects of Law Enforcement as it Affects the Single Homeless. A Submission from the Simon Community National Office to the Commission of Enquiry into the Irish Penal System* (Dublin: Simon Community, 1979).

138 Any given percentage reduction in crime requires a higher proportionate increase in the prison population because so many crimes go unreported, undetected or unconvicted. R. Tarling, *Analysing Offending: Data, Models and Interpretations* (London: HMSO, 1993); R. Tarling, 'The Effect of Imprisonment on Crime', *Journal of the Royal Statistical Society,* Series A, vol. 157, no. 2, 1994, pp. 173–76.

139 Criminal Legal Aid Review Committee, *First Report* (Dublin: Stationery Office, 1999), pp. 41–42.

140 For further information, see L. Wacquant, 'Suitable Enemies: Foreigners and Immigrants in the Prisons of Europe', *Punishment and Society: The International Journal of Penology*, vol. 1, no. 2, 1999, pp. 215–22.

141 S. Oppler, 'Assessing the State of South African Prisons', *African Security Review*, vol. 7, no. 4, 1998.

142 C. Murray, *Does Prison Work?* (London: Institute of Economic Affairs, 1997).

143 A. Beck, *Prison and Jail Inmates at Midyear 1999* (US Department of Justice/Bureau of Justice Statistics Bulletin, 2000).

144 Since the US Supreme Court ruled the death penalty constitutional in 1976, thirty-eight states have adopted new capital punishment statutes consistent with Supreme Court decisions on procedural guidelines. See J.H. Culver, 'Capital Punishment Politics and Policies in the States, 1977–1997', *Crime, Law and Social Change*, vol. 32, no. 4, 1999, pp. 287–300.

145 J. Savelsberg, 'Knowledge, Domination and Criminal Punishment', *American Journal of Sociology*, vol. 99, no. 4, 1994, pp. 919–20. Sutton argues that prison growth is driven not only by crime rates and unemployment rates, but also by the power of right-wing parties. J.R. Sutton, 'Imprisonment and Social Classification in Five Common Law Democracies 1955–1985', *American Journal of Sociology*, vol. 106, no. 2, 2000, pp. 350–86.

146 Parole refers to community supervision after a period of incarceration. Probation refers to court-ordered community supervision of
convicted offenders by a probation agency. Prison means confinement in a State or Federal correctional facility to serve a sentence of
more than one year. Jail means confinement in a local facility while
await trial, awaiting sentencing, serving a sentence that is usually
less than one year, or awaiting transfer to other facilities after conviction.

147 See also M. Tonry, *Malign Neglect: Race, Crime, and Punishment in
America* (New York: Oxford University Press, 1995).

148 S.R. Donziger (ed.), *The Real War on Crime: The Report of the National
Criminal Justice Commission* (New York: HarperPerennial, 1996).

149 B. Western and K. Beckett, 'How Unregulated is the US Labor
Market? The Penal System as a Labor Market Institution', *American
Journal of Sociology,* vol. 104, no. 4, 1999, pp. 1030–60.

150 J.P. Lynch and W.J. Sabol, 'Prison Use and Social Control', *Criminal
Justice 2000: Policies, Processes, and Decisions of the Criminal Justice
System* (Washington: US Department of Justice, 2000), p. 7.

151 K. Wolpin, 'An Economic Model of Crime and Punishment in England
and Wales 1894–1967', *Journal of Political Economy,* vol. 86, 1978, pp.
815–40.

152 S. Box, *Recession, Crime and Punishment* (London: Macmilllan, 1987).

153 T. Chiricos, 'Rates of Crime and Unemployment: An Analysis of
Aggregate Research Evidence', *Social Problems,* vol. 34, 1986, pp.
187–212.

154 D.P. Farrington et al., 'Unemployment, School Leaving and Crime',
*British Journal of Criminology,* vol. 26, no. 3, 1986, pp. 335–56.

155 C. Hale, 'The Labour Market and Post-War Crime Trends in England
and Wales', in P. Carlan and R. Morgan (eds.), *Crime Unlimited:
Questions for the 21st Century* (Macmillan: Basingstoke, 1997); C.
Hale, 'Crime and the Business Cycle in Post-War Britain Revisited',
*British Journal of Criminology,* vol. 38, 1998, pp. 681–98.

156 S. Field, *Trends in Crime and Their Interpretation: A Study of Recorded
Crime in Post-War England and Wales,* Home Office Research Study
119 (London: HMSO, 1990).

157 The Garda statistics show that in 36 per cent of larcenies recorded
during the first nine months of 1999 (and 21 per cent of burglaries
and robberies), the value of the property stolen was less than £100.
That the rewards associated with much property crime are so

modest would support the view that an increase in prosperity might reduce the motivation to offend in this way.

158 S. Field, *Trends in Crime and Their Interpretation: A Study of Recorded Crime in Post-War England and Wales*, Home Office Research Study 119 (London: HMSO, 1990), p. 5.

159 E. Dooley, *Homicide in Ireland 1972–1991* (Dublin: Stationery Office, 1995), p. 19.

160 The Quarterly National Household Survey indicates that in the twelve months to December – February 2000: employment increased by 95,600 or over 6 per cent; unemployment fell by about 13,600 to a rate of 4.7 per cent; and the long-term unemployment rate fell to 1.7 per cent. The rates of unemployment for males of the ages 15–19 and 20–24 were 9.6 and 5.6 per cent respectively at the end of 1999 compared to 20 and 15.7 per cent in 1997.

161 It should be stressed that the work by Field and others was limited to those offences which were recorded by the police. Thus it excluded the criminal activities of the middle classes, which tend to be hidden from the official record but can have devastating consequences. Improving economic conditions will increase the opportunities for such crimes. It would not be surprising, therefore, to find prosperity followed by an increase in the incidence of fraud, insider trading, health and safety violations in the workplace and so forth.

162 Field is not without his critics. His work has been condemned as 'atheoretical empiricism' by R. Matthews, *Doing Time: An Introduction to the Sociology of Punishment* (London: Macmillan, 1999), p. 108.

163 Council of Europe, *Crime and Economy,* Council of Europe Criminological Research Vol. XXXII (Strasbourg: Council of Europe, 1995).

164 In one of the only such studies in Ireland, a very weak relationship was found between the rate of imprisonment and the rate of unemployment. See C. McCullagh, 'Unemployment and Imprisonment: Examining and Interpreting the Relationship in the Republic of Ireland', *Irish Journal of Sociology*, vol. 2, 1992, pp. 1–19.

165 S.J. South, and S.F. Messner, 'Crime and Demography: Multiple Linkages, Reciprocal Relations', *Annual Review of Sociology*, vol. 26, 2000, p. 85.

166 M. Le Blanc and R. Loeber, 'Developmental Criminology Updates', in M. Tonry (ed.), *Crime and Justice – A Review of Research*, vol. 23 (University of Chicago Press, 1998).

167 S. Field, *Trends in Crime Revisited,* Home Office Research Study 195 (London: Home Office, 1999).

168 For a detailed review, see T. Seddon, 'Explaining the Drug–Crime Link: Theoretical, Policy and Research Issues', *Journal of Social Policy*, vol. 29, no. 1, 2000, pp. 95-108.

169 H.R. White and D.M. Gorman, 'Dynamics of the Drug–Crime Relationship', *Criminal Justice 2000: The Nature Of Crime: Continuity and Change* (Washington: US Department of Justice, 2000), p. 196.

170 C. Comiskey, *Estimating the Prevalence of Opiate Drug Use in Dublin, Ireland During 1996* (Dublin: Department of Health, 1998).

171 E. Keogh, *Illicit Drug Use and Related Criminal Activity in the Dublin Metropolitan Area* (Dublin: Garda Síochána, 1997).

172 M. Farrell, C. Gerada and J. Marsden, *External Review of Drug Services for the Eastern Health Board* (London: National Addiction Centre, Institute of Psychiatry, 2000).

173 J. Coid et al., *The Impact of Methadone Treatment on Drug Misuse and Crime,* Research Findings No. 120 (London: Home Office, 2000). J. Keen et al., 'Can Methadone Maintenance for Heroin-Dependent Patients Retained in General Practice Reduce Criminal Conviction Rates and Time Spent in Prison?', *British Journal of General Practice*, vol. 50, no. 450, 2000, pp. 48–9.

174 M. O'Neill and A.M. O'Connor, *Drug Using Women Working in Prostitution* (Dublin: Eastern Health Board, 1999), p. 10

175 M. Woods, 'Women, Drug Use and Parenting in Dublin: The Views of Professional Workers in the Drug Treatment and Social Work Fields', in A. Springer and A. Uhl (eds.), *Illicit Drugs: Patterns of Use – Patterns of Response* (Innsbruck: StudienVerlag, 2000).

176 For example see J. Mattinson and C. Mirrlees-Black, *Attitudes to Crime and Criminal Justice: Findings from the 1998 British Crime Survey,* Research Findings 111 (London: Home Office, 2000).

177 K. Beckett, *Making Crime Pay: Law and Order in Contemporary American Politics* (New York: Oxford University Press, 1997), p. 4.

178 ibid. p.4.

179 P. Tornudd, *Fifteen Years of Declining Prisoner Rates* (Helsinki: National Research Institute of Legal Policy, 1993).

180 T. Lappi-Seppala, *Regulating the Prison Population: Experiences From a Long-Term Policy in Finland* (Helsinki: National Research Institute of Legal Policy, 1998).

181 ibid. p. 108.

182 *Alternatives to Prison: Fine Gael Proposals for a Positive and Effective Approach to Crime* (Dublin: Fine Gael, 1998).

183 T. Caplow and J. Simon, 'Understanding Prison Policy and Population Trends', in M. Tonry and J. Petersilia (eds.), *Crime and Justice: An Annual Review of Research*, vol. 26 (University of Chicago Press, 1999).

184 D. Garland, 'The Limits of the Sovereign State: Strategies of Crime Control in Contemporary Society', *British Journal of Criminology*, vol. 36, no. 4, 1996, p. 446.

185 D. Garland, 'The Culture of High Crime Societies: Some Preconditions of Recent 'Law and Order' Policies', *British Journal of Criminology*, vol. 40, no. 3, 2000, pp. 347–75.

186 A number of measures to facilitate the seizure of criminal assets were enacted in the aftermath of these killings. They were: the Proceeds of Crime Act 1996; the Criminal Assets Bureau Act 1996; and the Disclosure of Certain information for Taxation and Other Purposes Act 1996. In combination, these new pieces of legislation considerably extended the reach of the law. For a discussion, see J.P. McCutcheon and D. Walsh (eds.), *The Confiscation of Criminal Assets: Law and Procedure* (Dublin: Round Hall Sweet and Maxwell, 1999).

187 S. Hall et al., *Policing the Crisis: Mugging, the State, and Law and Order* (London: Macmillan, 1978).

188 Expert Group on the Probation and Welfare Service, *Final Report* (Dublin: Stationery Office, 1999).

189 Sub-Committee on Crime and Punishment of the Joint Committee on Justice, Equality, Defence and Women's Rights, *Alternatives to Fines and the Uses of Prison* (Dublin: Houses of the Oireachtas, 2000).

190 The Forum was addressed by George Kelling and Catherine Coles, advocates of the 'broken windows' approach to crime prevention. Chapter 12 of the Forum's report addresses the question of 'zero tolerance', which is described as a phrase not much used by criminologists 'who had a feel for accuracy' (p. 164).

191 This appears to be in stark contrast to the UK, where it has been argued that 'there has been considerable and steadily increasing public support for stricter and more punitive penal policies'. See G. Johnstone, 'Penal Policy Making: Elitist, Populist or Participatory?', *Punishment and Society: The International Journal of Penology*, vol. 2, no. 2, 2000, p. 164.

192 National Crime Forum, *Report* (Dublin: Institute of Public Administration, 1998), p. 142.

193 N. Christie, *Crime Control as Industry: Towards Gulags, Western Style* (London: Routledge, 1993), p. 16.

194 D. Garland, *Punishment and Modern Society* (University of Chicago Press, 1990), p. 20.

# Select Bibliography

An Garda Síochána (2000) *Annual Report on Crime 1999.* Dublin: Stationery Office.

Bacik, I. and O'Connell, M. (eds) *Crime and Poverty in Ireland.* Dublin: Round Hall Sweet and Maxwell.

Beckett, K. (1997) *Making Crime Pay: Law and Order in Contemporary American Politics.* New York: Oxford University Press.

Bratton, W. and Knobler, P. (1998) *Turnaround: How America's Top Cop Reversed the Crime Epidemic.* New York: Random House.

Brewer, J.D., Lockhart, B. and Rodgers, P. (1997) *Crime in Ireland, 1945–95: Here be Dragons.* Oxford: Clarendon Press.

Caplow, T. and Simon, J. (1999) 'Understanding Prison Policy and Population Trends' in Tonry, M. and Petersilia, J. (eds) *Crime and Justice: An Annual Review of Research, Vol. 26.* University of Chicago Press.

Central Statistcs Office (1999) *Quarterly National Household Survey – Crime and Victimisation.* Dublin: CSO.

Coleman, C. and Moynihan, J. (1996) *Understanding Crime Data: Haunted by the Dark Figure.* Milton Keynes: Open University Press.

Dennis, N. (ed) (1998) *Zero Tolerance: Policing a Free Society.* London: Institute of Economic Affairs.

Department of Justice (1994) *The Management Of Offenders: A Five-Year Plan.* Dublin: Stationery Office.

Department of Justice (1997) *Tackling Crime: A Discussion Paper.* Dublin: Stationery Office.

Department of Justice, Equality and Law Reform (1999) *Final Report of the Expert Group on the Probation and Welfare Service.* Dublin: Stationery Office.

Donziger, S.R. (1996) (ed) *The Real War on Crime: The Report of the National Criminal Justice Commission.* New York: HarperPerennial.

Fennell, C. (1993) *Crime and Crisis in Ireland: Justice by Illusion.* Cork University Press.

Fianna Fáil (1997) *Leading the Fight against Crime: A Fianna Fáil Position Paper on Justice.*

Field, S. (1999) *Trends in Crime Revisited.* Home Office Research Study 195. London: Home Office.

Garland, D. (2000) 'The Culture of High Crime Societies: Some Preconditions of Recent "Law and Order" Policies'. *British Journal of Criminology*, vol, 40, No. 1, pp. 347–75.

Kelling, R. and Coles, C. (1996) *Fixing Broken Windows: Restoring and Reducing Crime in Our Communities*. New York: Free Press.

McCullagh, C. (1996) *Crime in Ireland: A Sociological Introduction*. Cork University Press.

Murray, C. (1997) *Does Prison Work?* London: Institute of Economic Affairs.

National Crime Forum (1998) *Report*. Dublin: Institute of Public Administration.

Nelken, D. (1997) 'White Collar Crime' in Maguire, M., Morgan, R. and Reiner, R. (eds) *The Oxford Handbook of Criminology*. Oxford University Press.

O'Connell, M. (1999) 'Is Irish Public Opinion towards Crime Distorted by Media Bias?' *European Journal of Communication,* Vol. 14, No. 2, pp. 191–212.

O'Mahony, P. (2000) *Prison Policy in Ireland: Criminal Justice versus Social Justice*. Cork University Press.

Parenti, C. (1999) *Lockdown America: Police and Prisons in the Age of Crisis*. New York: Verso.

Reiner, R. (2000) Crime and Control in Britain. *Sociology,* Vol. 34, No.1, pp. 71–94.

Rottman, D.B. (1980) *Crime in the Republic of Ireland: Statistical Trends and their Interpretation.* Paper No. 102. Dublin: Economic and Social Research Institute.

Sub-Committee on Crime and Punishment of the Joint Committee on Justice, Equality, Defence and Women's Rights (2000) *Alternatives to Fines and the Uses of Prison.* Dublin: Houses of the Oireachtas.

Steering Group on the Efficiency and Effectiveness of the Garda Síochána. (1997) *Report.* Dublin: Stationery Office.

Tarling R. (1994) 'The Effect of Imprisonment on Crime'. *Journal of the Royal Statistical Society, Series A*, 157(2), pp. 173–76.

Watson, D. (2000) *Victims of Recorded Crime in Ireland: Results from the 1996 Survey.* Dublin: ESRI/Oaktree Press.

Young, J. (1999) *The Exclusive Society: Social Exclusion, Crime and Difference in Late Modernity.* London: Sage.